Communications
in Computer and Information Science 1634

More information about this series at https://link.springer.com/bookseries/7899

Enzo Rucci · Marcelo Naiouf ·
Franco Chichizola · Laura De Giusti ·
Armando De Giusti (Eds.)

Cloud Computing, Big Data & Emerging Topics

10th Conference, JCC-BD&ET 2022
La Plata, Argentina, June 28–30, 2022
Proceedings

Springer

Editors
Enzo Rucci ⓘ
National University of La Plata
La Plata, Argentina

Marcelo Naiouf ⓘ
National University of La Plata
La Plata, Argentina

Franco Chichizola ⓘ
National University of La Plata
La Plata, Argentina

Laura De Giusti ⓘ
National University of La Plata
La Plata, Argentina

Armando De Giusti ⓘ
National University of La Plata
La Plata, Argentina

ISSN 1865-0929   ISSN 1865-0937 (electronic)
Communications in Computer and Information Science
ISBN 978-3-031-14598-8   ISBN 978-3-031-14599-5 (eBook)
https://doi.org/10.1007/978-3-031-14599-5

This Springer imprint is published by the registered company Springer Nature Switzerland AG
The registered company address is: Gewerbestrasse 11, 6330 Cham, Switzerland

Preface

Welcome to the proceedings of the 10th Conference on Cloud Computing, Big Data & Emerging Topics (JCC-BD&ET 2022), held in a hybrid setting (with both on-site and live online participation modes) during June 28–30, 2022. JCC-BD&ET 2022 was organized by the III-LIDI and the Postgraduate Office of the School of Computer Science, National University of La Plata, Argentina.

Since 2013, this event has been an annual meeting where ideas, projects, scientific results, and applications in the cloud computing, big data, and other related areas are exchanged and disseminated. The conference focuses on the topics that allow interaction between academia, industry, and other interested parties.

JCC-BD&ET 2022 covered the following topics: cloud, edge, fog, accelerator, green, web, and mobile computing; big and open data; machine and deep learning; smart and sustainable cities; and special topics related to emerging technologies. In addition, it featured special activities including a plenary lecture and a discussion panel.

In this edition, the conference received 23 submissions. The authors of these submissions came from the following seven countries: Argentina, Chile, Colombia, Ecuador, India, Paraguay, and Spain. All the accepted papers were peer reviewed by at least three referees (single-blind review) and evaluated on the basis of technical quality, relevance, significance, and clarity. To achieve this, JCC-BD&ET 2022 was supported by 51 Program Committee (PC) members and 31 additional external reviewers. According to the recommendations of the referees, nine of the papers were selected for this book (39% acceptance rate). We hope readers will find these contributions useful and inspiring for their future research.

Special thanks go to all the people who contributed to the conference's success: Program and Organizing Committee members, authors, reviewers, speakers, and all conference attendees. Finally, we want to thank Springer for its support in publishing this book.

June 2022

Enzo Rucci
Marcelo Naiouf
Franco Chichizola
Laura De Giusti
Armando De Giusti

Organization

General Chair

Marcelo Naiouf   Universidad Nacional de La Plata, Argentina

Program Committee Chairs

Armando De Giusti   Universidad Nacional de La Plata and CONICET,
                                Argentina
Franco Chichizola   Universidad Nacional de La Plata, Argentina
Laura De Giusti   Universidad Nacional de La Plata and CIC,
                                Argentina
Enzo Rucci   Universidad Nacional de La Plata and CIC,
                                Argentina

Program Committee

María José Abásolo   Universidad Nacional de La Plata and CIC,
                                Argentina
José Aguilar   Universidad de Los Andes, Venezuela
Jorge Ardenghi   Universidad Nacional del Sur, Argentina
Javier Balladini   Universidad Nacional del Comahue, Argentina
Oscar Bria   Universidad Nacional de La Plata and INVAP,
                                Argentina
Silvia Castro   Universidad Nacional del Sur, Argentina
Mónica Denham   Universidad Nacional de Río Negro and
                                CONICET, Argentina
Javier Diaz   Universidad Nacional de La Plata, Argentina
Ramón Doallo   Universidade da Coruña, Spain
Marcelo Errecalde   Universidad Nacional de San Luis, Argentina
Elsa Estevez   Universidad Nacional del Sur and CONICET,
                                Argentina
Aurelio Fernandez Bariviera   Universitat Rovira i Virgili, Spain
Héctor Florez Fernández   Universidad Distrital Francisco José de Caldas,
                                Colombia
Fernando Emmanuel Frati   Universidad Nacional de Chilecito, Argentina
Carlos Garcia Garino   Universidad Nacional de Cuyo, Argentina
Carlos García Sánchez   Universidad Complutense de Madrid, Spain

Adriana Angélica Gaudiani	Universidad Nacional de General Sarmiento, Argentina
Graciela Verónica Gil Costa	Universidad Nacional de San Luis and CONICET, Argentina
Roberto Guerrero	Universidad Nacional de San Luis, Argentina
Waldo Hasperué	Universidad Nacional de La Plata and CIC, Argentina
Francisco Daniel Igual Peña	Universidad Complutense de Madrid, Spain
Tomasz Janowski	Gdansk University of Technology, Poland
Laura Lanzarini	Universidad Nacional de La Plata, Argentina
Guillermo Leguizamón	Universidad Nacional de San Luis, Argentina
Edimara Luciano	Pontificia Universidade Católica do Rio Grande do Sul, Brazil
Emilio Luque Fadón	Universidad Autónoma de Barcelona, Spain
Mauricio Marín	Universidad de Santiago de Chile, Chile
Luis Marrone	Universidad Nacional de La Plata, Argentina
Katzalin Olcoz Herrero	Universidad Complutense de Madrid, Spain
José Angel Olivas Varela	Universidad de Castilla-La Mancha, Spain
Xoan Pardo	Universidade da Coruña, Spain
Patricia Pesado	Universidad Nacional de La Plata, Argentina
María Fabiana Piccoli	Universidad Nacional de San Luis, Argentina
Luis Piñuel	Universidad Complutense de Madrid, Spain
Adrian Pousa	Universidad Nacional de La Plata, Argentina
Marcela Printista	Universidad Nacional de San Luis, Argentina
Dolores Isabel Rexachs del Rosario	Universidad Autónoma de Barcelona, Spain
Nelson Rodríguez	Universidad Nacional de San Juan, Argentina
Juan Carlos Saez Alcaide	Universidad Complutense de Madrid, Spain
Aurora Sánchez	Universidad Católica del Norte, Chile
Victoria Sanz	Universidad Nacional de La Plata, Argentina
Remo Suppi	Universidad Autónoma de Barcelona, Spain
Francisco Tirado Fernández	Universidad Complutense de Madrid, Spain
Juan Touriño Dominguez	Universidade da Coruña, Spain
Gabriela Viale Pereira	Danube University Krems, Austria
Gonzalo Zarza	Globant, Argentina

Additional Reviewers

Nelson Acosta	Alejandra Cechich
Pedro Alvarez	Cecilia Challiol
Rubén Apolloni	Leonardo Corbalan
Sandra Baldasarri	César Estrebou
Ricardo Barrientos	Alejandro Fernandez

Pablo Fillottrani
Luján Ganuza
Mario Alejandro García
Wenny Hojas-Mazo
Jorge Ierache
Martín Larrea
Cristina Manresa-Yee
Antonio Navarro Martín
Ariel Pasini
David Petrocelli
Claudia Pons

Hugo Ramón
Franco Ronchetti
Gustavo Rossi
Gustavo Salazar
Cecilia Sanz
Matías Selzer
Dana Urribarri
Augusto Villa Monte
Gonzalo Luján Villarreal
Alejandro Zunino

Sponsors

Sistema Nacional
de Computación
de Alto Desempe-
ño

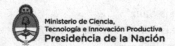

Ministerio de Ciencia,
Tecnología e Innovación Productiva
Presidencia de la Nación

RedUNCI

Agencia Nacional de Promoción
Científica y Tecnológica

Red de Universidades Nacionales
con Carreras de Informática

Contents

Virtual Reality

Cloud and High-Performance Computing

File Access Patterns of Distributed Deep Learning Applications

Edixon Parraga[1]([✉])(iD), Betzabeth Leon[1](iD), Sandra Mendez[1,2](iD),
Dolores Rexachs[1](iD), and Emilio Luque[1](iD)

[1] Computer Architecture and Operating Systems Department,
Universitat Autónoma de Barcelona, 08193 Bellaterra, Barcelona, Spain
{edixon.parraga,betzabeth.leon,sandra.mendez,
dolores.rexachs,emilio.luque}@uab.es
[2] Computer Sciences Department, Barcelona Supercomputing Center (BSC),
08034 Barcelona, Spain
sandra.mendez@bsc.es

Abstract. Nowadays, Deep Learning (DL) applications have become a necessary solution for analyzing and making predictions with big data in several areas. However, DL applications introduce heavy input/output (I/O) loads on computer systems. These types of applications, when running on distributed systems or distributed memory parallel systems, handle a large amount of information that must be read in the training stage. Inherently parallel and distributed systems and persistent file accesses can easily overwhelm traditional shared file systems and negatively impact application performance. In this way, the management of these applications constitutes a constant challenge due to their popularity in HPC systems. Scientific applications or simulators have traditionally been executed and are optimized for this type systems. Therefore, it is essential to identify the key factors involved in the I/O of a DL application to find the most appropriate form of configuration to minimize the impact of I/O on the performance of this type of application. In the present work, we present an analysis of the behavior of the patterns generated by I/O operations in the training stage of distributed deep learning applications. We selected two well-known datasets such as CIFAR and MNIST to describe file access patterns.

Keywords: Distributed deep learning · High performance computing · File input/Output · Parallel I/O

1 Introduction

In recent years, Deep Learning (DL) has drawn much attention due to its potential usefulness in different types of applications in the real world. Basic param-

This publication is supported under contract PID2020-112496GB-I00, funded by the Agencia Estatal de Investigación (AEI), Spain and the Fondo Europeo de Desarrollo Regional (FEDER) UE and partially funded by a research collaboration agreement with the Fundación Escuelas Universitarias Gimbernat (EUG).

E. Rucci et al. (Eds.): JCC-BD&ET 2022, CCIS 1634, pp. 3–19, 2022.
https://doi.org/10.1007/978-3-031-14599-5_1

eters about the data are configured, and the computer is trained to learn on its own. It recognizes patterns by using many layers of processing, managing large volumes of data for the training of a model, through which predictions can be made.

The ingestion of this massive amount of information needed to train networks means that high-performance computing (HPC) requires handling large amounts of data and it is not limited to traditional workloads such as simulation [14]. DL applications introduce heavy I/O loads with long, highly simultaneous, and persistent file access, which can overwhelm the conventional file system. Thus, for data-intensive DL applications, I/O performance can become a bottleneck that generates high training latency and introduces CPU and memory overhead, especially when datasets are too large to fit in memory.

Some of the most popular deep-learning uses include speech recognition, natural language processing, image recognition, recommendation systems, amongst other things. This vast difference in the information that feeds these systems results in a diverse set of I/O patterns that differ from traditional HPC I/O behavior [14]. Therefore, the way to treat this information must also be different, adapted to the needs of variability, randomness, frequency, and repetitive use that these deep learning applications and training from datasets with these characteristics naturally have.

Since the training stage requires a large number of computing resources, there are several proposals in the literature to improve the performance of DL applications [13]. However, there are still many areas to be developed, especially regarding I/O, due to its complexity. In this way, in the present work, we present a methodology for analyzing the behavior of input/output file access patterns of DL applications in distributed systems. We will focus on two well-known datasets such as CIFAR and MNIST, which can be handled with few resources, in order to carry out a detailed analysis at small scale of the behavior of the patterns generated in the I/O operations in the training stage.

This paper is structured as follows: Sect. 2 presents related work. Section 3 characterizes the I/O Patterns Models of DL applications. Section 4 shows experimental data-extraction for file I/O pattern modelling characterization. Finally, in Sect. 5, we explain our conclusions and future work.

2   Related Work

In the literature, several studies have been carried out around the characterization of the I/O from different perspectives. For example, in [14], the authors provided a systematic I/O description of ML I/O jobs to understand both how I/O behavior differs across several scientific domains and the scale of workloads. They studied the use of the parallel and burst file system per ML I/O jobs. Furthermore, in [8,20], the authors carried out an analysis of the bottleneck generated by the I/O in the training phase of machine learning. This analysis includes access patterns and a performance model that gives us an overview of storage strategies and their influence on I/O. In the first one, the authors introduced NoPFS, a machine learning I/O middleware and in the second one the authors presented a design DeepIO, an I/O framework for training deep neural networks. Likewise, in [18], the authors designed and built prediction models to estimate performance degradation due to workload placement.

On the other hand, in [17], the authors formulated the prediction of I/O performance in production HPC systems as a classification problem and used machine learning techniques to address it. This paper states that storage sub-systems are complex, and the I/O operations of running applications can have irregular patterns. In [21] and [9], the authors also dealt with the analysis of access patterns. In the first paper, the I/O patterns of deep neural networks were examined, and in the second, a deep recurrent neural network was proposed that learns the patterns of I/O requests and predicts the next ones.

Regarding the behavior of HPC applications using different file systems, formats, and libraries, [5,22] compared the I/O load performance of an HPC application on several file systems. Parallel libraries like HDF5, PnetCDF, and MPI-IO were used to attain their I/O patterns. Likewise, in [19], the authors showed the essential characteristics that file systems must have so that they can meet the needs of DL applications.

Moreover, in [3], the authors studied some of the most used frameworks, because they indicate that deep learning systems suffer from scalability limitations, particularly for data I/O. These studies characterized the I/O performance and scaling of different frameworks. Likewise, the authors carried out an analysis of the I/O subsystem to understand the cause of its inefficiency.

As can be seen from the literature cited in this section, the authors proposed solutions to introduce new middle-ware, I/O frameworks, file system, file format analysis, burst buffer usage, and various prediction models. With our work in this first phase of the research, we intend to analyze the file access patterns of distributed deep learning applications.

Compared to the research cited in this section, our contribution is that we intend to determine the influence of the variability of various parameters·and techniques that could impact the I/O of DL applications. This is an analysis of the temporal and spatial behavior, taking into account the phases of I/O as groupings of the behavior. With this information, a user could recognize the problem and decide to use configuration strategies that allow I/O to have less impact on DL applications.

3 Characterizing the I/O Patterns Models of DDL Applications

3.1 Software Stack DL

A software stack consists of all the software components necessary to support the execution of the application. The components of a software stack work together to deliver application services to the end-user efficiently. The DL application I/O software stack is different from the traditional I/O software stack used in HPC. As shown in Fig. 1, the applications are located at the top, which will go through other layers necessary for its operation, in which the frameworks and libraries are found. The most used frameworks are Tensorflow [2], Pytorch [1], Caffe [10] and, for distributed DL, Horovod [16]. Then there is the file system with all the elements associated with it, which can directly impact the pattern of access to files concerning the behavior of I/O operations. This lower layers are related to the logical relationship between hardware and software, such as I/O buffers, controllers, and the disks on which the information is stored.

It is important to know the I/O software stack on which we are working to know which monitoring tools should be used. In addition, it is essential to know at which level of the stack to observe the specific behavior of each layer that can affect the access patterns to files of the DL applications.

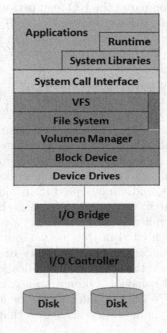

Fig. 1. Deep learning - IO software stack

3.2   File Access Pattern

In the present work, we will focus on the training phase of DL applications. Thus, this section briefly describes the training stage, specifying its close relationship with the I/O when reading the datasets. The purpose is to improve the understanding of the moment in which the I/O operations occur to a greater extent and, therefore, where the I/O pattern of file access can be analyzed.

DL applications work through deep neural networks, grouped into input layers that receive the data and hidden layers that perform the mathematical calculations. The model is fitted to the training dataset; this function trains the model for a fixed number of epochs. In this phase, the dataset information is read, and checkpoints [15] are generated according to the configuration used. After this training, an evaluation is performed to confirm that the model is working as desired. Once the model has been successfully evaluated, predictions can be made. There are two essential elements to consider: a large amount of computing power and a large amount of data to train the network correctly.

Deep learning applications introduce heavy I/O loads on computing systems regarding a large amount of training data. Distributed DL file data access is highly concurrent and persists throughout the training process. The features of files vary from many small files or one very large shared file [19]. This situation can easily overwhelm traditional shared file systems and negatively impact application performance. When considering the types of parallel I/O, there are two types, as shown in Fig. 2. One file per process, which is more straightforward, and where each process generates its own file. All access to the files is done independently, so no synchronization is needed between I/O operations. In the case of the shared file, all the processes access a single file, which has advantages in disk storage space.

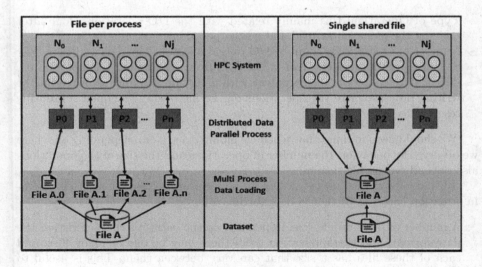

Fig. 2. Training stage - Dataset access

In addition to the types of file I/O access, it should be noted that if the datasets are small, the system cache or local node storage, such as an SSD, might hold the entire dataset and not affect performance. However, if they are substantial datasets that do not fit in the file system cache or local node storage, they could affect the performance of the learning workload due to the resulting bottleneck [4]. In this way, new technologies and methodologies have had to be incorporated to manage all the information of these applications.

The file access pattern is helpful to being able to make predictions and thus being able to optimize the execution of the application by configuring several parameters. The access pattern can be spatial and temporal.

– Spatial pattern: this indicates how the file is being accessed taking into account the file offset and the request size.
– Temporal pattern: this shows how processes are accessing the file during the application's execution.

Figure 3 depicts the key I/O characteristics that we consider to model the file access patterns of DL applications running on HPC. We divide this characteristics in two main groups as follows:

– Data Access: it is mainly related with the information needed to represent the spatial and temporal I/O patterns for each file open by a DL application.
– Meta-information: it related with the information need to understand the usefulness of the file for the whole application and to determine the I/O resources required by the files of a DL application.

The information related with the **data access** is described as follows:

– Type of Operation: this mainly related with the I/O operations done after opening the file, such as read and write operations.
– Number of Operations: count of I/O operations done to/from a file.
– Size of Operations: bytes wrote to or read from a file by an I/O operation.
– Offset: it refers to the displacement within the file, it indicates a reading or writing process where the operations on the file begin. The open subroutine resets it to 0.

We should keep in mind that when we monitor a system, depending on where we observe the behavior, the number of operations and the size of the operations also depend on the file system.

To understand the I/O context of an application we also consider the meta-information (See Fig. 3) that is described as follows:

– A number of files and file size: Depending on the dataset's characteristics, the data format, and the application used, there may be one or many files, and each of these files has a size that can vary between them. This is useful to know the I/O resources required by an application.
– Type of Access: The type of access can be read-only, write-only, or open for read/write.
– File Type: When the file type is shared, all processes access a single file. A different kind of file is when each process accesses it independently, so there is no need for synchronization between I/O operations; one file is accessed per process.
– Access mode: it can be random, sequential, or strided.

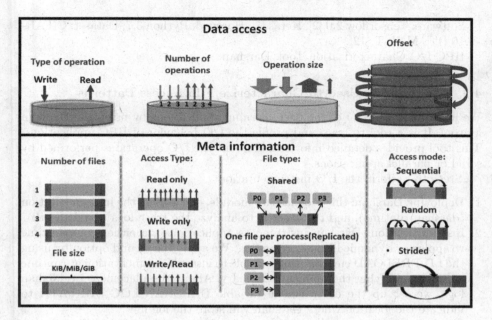

Fig. 3. File access pattern and meta information

The behavior does not necessarily have to be unique throughout the entire application's execution, but taking into account the temporal pattern, we can distinguish phases with different spatial behavior. A phase is temporarily identified during a time interval and it is described by its spatial pattern. This behavior can be repeated throughout the application. In the next phase, it can have a different spatial pattern.

4 Experimental Data-extraction for File Access Pattern Modelling Characterization

In this section, we present the experimental Data-extraction for file access pattern modelling characterization. A benchmark that trains a neural network for pattern recognition was used. It was executed with 1, 4, and 8 processes in a single node.

4.1 Experimental Environment

The technical description of experimental environments is as follows:

– Compute nodes - Processor Haswell 2680v3, Intel(R) Xeon(R) CPU E5-2680 v3 @ 2.50 GHz, 24 CORES, 128 GB of RAM.
– I/O systems: LUSTRE, NFS

– Software: Tensorflow 2.0 [2], Keras [7], Horovod, Python 3.7, Dataset: CIFAR-10 [11], MNIST [12].
– HPC I/O Characterization Tool: Darshan.

4.2   Mechanisms Used to Characterize File Access Patterns

We instrument the I/O of the deep learning applications by using the Darshan [6] tool. It is a tool to trace and profile the I/O behavior of HPC applications. This tool provides detailed information about the I/O operations performed by serial or parallel applications.

Steps to perform the I/O instrumentation:

1. Deploying Darshan: this tool has two module, one is to do the instrumentation (darshan-runtime), and the other is to analyze the trace logs (darshan-util).
2. Instrumentation: Darshan instruments applications via either compile time wrappers or dynamic library preloading. We apply the second option by using the LD_PRELOAD environment variable to insert instrumentation at runtime without modifying the application binary. About the placement of darshan logs, we set up the environment variable DARSHAN_LOG_DIR_PATH to indicate the location where Darshan will store the log files.
3. Darshan report generation and analysis: To have the whole I/O information of the application, we use the profile provided by Darshan. Part of the information obtained per job when run an application with Darshan is: total numbers of files, total read and write operations, maximum displacement, operation size grouped by ranges, time spent in operations, and so on. To have the information to represent the spatial and temporal pattern per file we enable the Darshan eXtended Tracing (DXT) module, because we need detailed information about the operation order, offset and request size.

4.3   Characterization of File Access Patterns to the CIFAR-10 Dataset

CIFAR-10 (a natural image data set with ten categories) consists of 60,000 32×32 color images in 10 classes, with 6,000 images per class. There are 50,000 training images and 10,000 test images. The dataset is divided into five training batches and one test batch containing 10,000 images. The test batch contains exactly 1,000 randomly selected images from each class. The training batches contain the remaining images in random order; the training batches contain exactly 5000 images of each class. The classes are mutually exclusive; the same picture cannot belong to more than one class.

The results of the experimentation with CIFAR-10 with four processes in a node on two file systems LUSTRE and NFS will be shown below, since the behavior varies according to the number and size of the operations.

Figure 4 shows the spatial pattern of access to a file (data batch 1) on LUSTRE. Thus, we observe the following:

– Type of Operation: read-only.

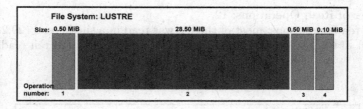

Fig. 4. Spatial pattern of access to 1 file (data_batch_1). Shared file (Dataset: Cifar10, File size: 29.6 MiB) File System:LUSTRE

- Number of Read Operations: 4.
- Size of read operations: most of the file was read in a single read (28.50 MiB); the rest of the reads were smaller, one at the beginning and two at the end.

As can be seen in Fig. 5, all the files of the dataset are accessed by one process. The small reads are shown at the beginning of the first operation of 512 kiB. Then, a large operation of 29184 kiB follows and ends with two small reads, one of 512 KiB and the last one 100.30 KiB. Let us remember that the CIFAR10 dataset is made up of five files called data_batch and a test_batch file, where we can see that this pattern is repeated for all the dataset files.

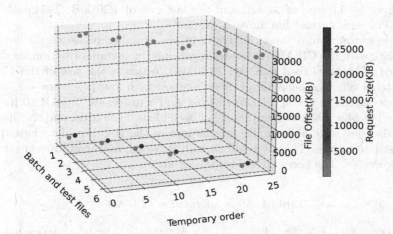

Fig. 5. Spatial and temporal pattern for a process. Each process open files in order starting from data_batch_1 to data_batch_5 and finally the test_batch. Each process read whole files following the same I/O pattern. Dataset: Cifar10, File size: 29.6MiB, and File System: LUSTRE.

Figure 6 shows the spatial pattern of access to a file (data batch 1) on NFS. Thus, we observe the following:

- Type of Operation: read-only.

- Number of Read Operations: 12.
- Size of read operations: most of the file was read in a single read (29.28 MiB), the rest of the reads were smaller, one at the beginning and ten reads at the end.

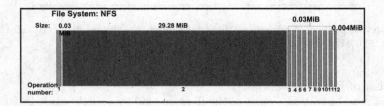

Fig. 6. Spatial pattern of access to 1 file (data_batch_1). Shared file (Dataset: Cifar10, File size: 29.6MiB)) File system:NFS

Figure 7 depicts the temporal and spatial pattern for CIFAR in a NFS file system. We can observe the view for a process, where all the dataset files are accessed, with a total of 12 read operations per file. These operations are distributed as follows: starts with a read operation of 32 kiB, after that a read of 29984 KiB, this follows by 11 read of 32 kiB and the last one of 4.30 kiB. This pattern is repeated in each dataset file for each process.

I/O operations have been analyzed in the training phase of the selected benchmark with the CIFAR-10 dataset regarding the metainformation, as shown in Table 1. The total read size was 29.60MiB, which is the size of the CIFAR data_batch_1 file. The behavior of this execution with four processes was similar to the executions of the application with 1 and 8 processes. CIFAR-10 has five data batches plus a test batch; the size of each file is 29.60 MiB, and the file type is shared. They were also similar for the rest of the training (data_batch) and test (test_batch) files. They were all shared, accessed, and read in their entirety by all processes. The access mode is sequential.

Table 1. Meta information - CIFAR

Number of files	File size	Files	Access type	File type	Access mode
6	29.6 MiB	Data_batch_1	Read only	Shared	Sequential
		Data_batch_2			
		Data_batch_3			
		Data_batch_4			
		Data_batch_5			
		Test_batch			

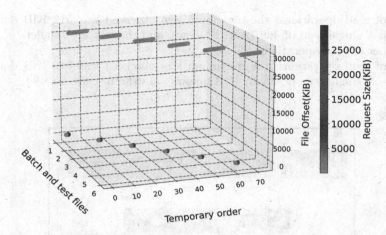

Fig. 7. Spatial and temporal pattern for a process. Each process open files in order starting from data_batch_1 to data_batch_5 and finally the test_batch. Each process read whole files following the same I/O pattern. Dataset: Cifar10, File size: 29.6MiB and File System:NFS

4.4 Characterization of File Access Patterns to the MNIST Dataset

MNIST is a dataset of 60,000 10-digit 28×28 grayscale images and a test set of 10,000 images. It is a subset of a larger set available from NIST. Handwritten digits are normalized in size and centered on a fixed-size image. They are composed of small images that facilitate rapid experimentation.

Figure 8 shows the spatial pattern of access to a file (mnist-0.npz), on LUSTRE. Thus, we observe the following:

– when the application is executed with a single process, and the dataset is stored on disk, it only reads the dataset (Fig. 8-A),
– but when the number of processes is increased, the dataset is replicated by performing write and read operations (Fig. 8-B).

In this way, when all the processes already have their files stored on disk, it presents the following behavior:

– Type of Operation: read-only.
– Number of read operations: 53.
– Size of read operations: the maximum size observed was 512 KiB done 44 times. A single read of 469.19 KiB follows, and the rest are smaller.

On the other hand, when the file must be replicated for each process, it presents the following behavior:

– Type of Operation: write/read.
– Number of write operations: 22.

- Size of read operations: the maximum size observed was 512 KiB done 21 times. A single read of 469.19 KiB follows, and the rest are smaller.
- Number of read operations: 29.
- Size of read operations: the maximum size observed was 512 KiB done 23 times. A single read of 409.02 KiB follows, and the rest are smaller.

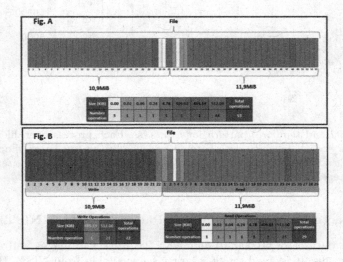

Fig. 8. Spatial pattern of access to 1 file (mnist-0.npz). (Dataset: MNIST, File size: 10.9MiB)) File System:LUSTRE

The MNIST dataset is made up of a single file. When run with a single process, the process accesses the file by performing fifty-three read operations. This temporal behavior is shown in Fig. 9a, where from operation one to fifty-two, it reads 512 KiB. First, finding in operation twenty-two a reading of 469.19 KiB, then in operations twenty-three, twenty-four, and twenty-seven with 0 bytes. Next, operation twenty-six of 22 bytes, followed by operation twenty-eight of 42 bytes. Then the operation twenty-nine of 248 bytes. Finally, operation forty-eight with 409.02 KiB ends at operation fifty-three with 4.78 KiB.

Figure 9b depicts the I/O pattern when the application is run with more than one process. It generates a file for each process. The observed pattern presents twenty-two write operations distributed from operation one to operation twenty-one with a write of 512 kiB. In the last twenty-two operations, it generates a write with 469.19 KiB. When it finishes performing the write operations, it performs twenty-nine read operations. These read operations are composed in a pattern similar to the previous figure, but in this case, it start with a large 512 kiB operation. Then operation number two with 22 bytes, operation number three with 0 bytes, operation number four with 42 bytes, and operation number five with 248 bytes. Then with large operations from operation six to twenty-eight with 512 KiB. Operation twenty-four with 409.02 KiB and closing the operation with a reading of 4.78 KiB.

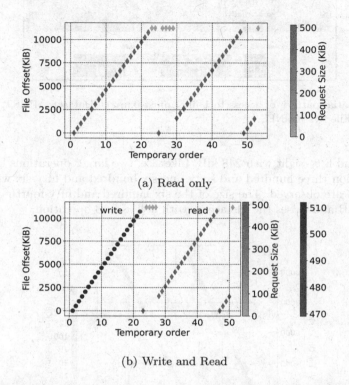

(a) Read only

(b) Write and Read

Fig. 9. Spatial and Temporal pattern for mnist-0.npz file. Dataset: MNIST, File size: 10.9MiB and File System:LUSTRE.

Figure 10 shows the spatial pattern of the `mnist-0.npz` file, in NFS when all dataset files for each process are stored on disk. Thus, we observe the following:

- Type of Operation: read-only.
- Number of read operations: 700.
- Size of read operations: the maximum size observed was 192 KiB done 2 times. 689 reads of 32 KiB follow, and the rest are smaller.

The application read/write files from/to a NFS file system; it performs 700 read operations on the MNIST dataset. Figure 11 shows the spatial and temporal I/O pattern. Operation one through operation number six hundred and ninety-nine are operations of size 32 KiB. Different sizes of read operations are generated throughout execution. Operation three hundred and fifty-one is of 21.13 kiB. The operations three hundred fifty-two, three hundred fifty-three, and three hundred fifty-six with 0 bytes. Operation three hundred and fifty-five with 22 bytes, and in operation three hundred and fifty-seven with 42 bytes. Then in the three

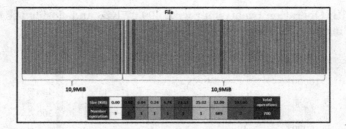

Fig. 10. Spatial pattern of access to 1 file (mnist-0.npz). (Dataset: MNIST, File size: 10.9MiB)) File System:NFS

hundred and fifty-eight with 248 kiB. Likewise, two larger operations located in the operation three hundred and sixty and six hundred and fifty-six with a size of 192 KiB are observed. The size of the six hundred and fifty-fourth operation is 25.02 KiB and closes the file access with a 4.78 KiB operation.

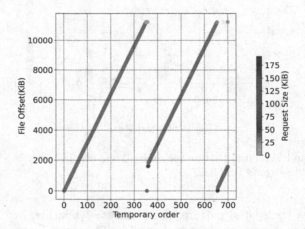

Fig. 11. Spatial and Temporal I/O pattern for the `mnist-0.npz` file. Dataset: MNIST, File size: 10.9MiN and File System: NFS

Regarding the metadata, as shown in Table 2, MNIST has one file, with a size of 10.9 MiB, the file type is replicated. This experiment analyzed what happens in the training phase of the benchmark on the readings made in MNIST. In this way, it was observed that each process accessed its own copy of the file. Therefore, it replicates the file in as many processes as are used. The access mode is sequential. As the file is replicated by the number of executed processes, write operations are also observed in order to be able to create these copies of dataset files. After creating all the files, access is read-only for each of them to train the model.

Table 2. Meta information - MNIST

Number of files	File size	Files	Access type	File type	Access mode
1 per process	10.9 MiB	mnist_0.npz	Read/Write	Replicated	Sequential
		mnist_1.npz			
		mnist_2.npz			
		mnist_3.npz			

In Fig. 12a we observe how each process accesses to the whole file. It has a greater number of small read operations (light green color) and two large ones with 700 operations in NFS file systems. Whereas in Fig. 12b read operations are larger (blue color) and a few smaller ones until completing the 53 operations in the LUSTRE file system.

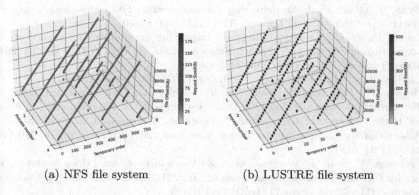

(a) NFS file system   (b) LUSTRE file system

Fig. 12. Spatial and temporal I/O Pattern by running with four processes for the MNIST dataset. Each process access its own dataset copy named `mnist-#PROC.npz`, where `#PROC` corresponds to process rank and each file copy is of 10.9 MiB.

5 Conclusions

In the present study, we have focused on analyzing the I/O patterns of access to files with the Tensorflow and Horovod framework for distributed executions. An analysis was carried out of the I/O patterns generated from the same application with 1, 4, and 8 processes in a node and on two different file systems such as LUSTRE and NFS. In this sense, it was observed that when the file system changed, the behavior of the access patterns changed in terms of the number and size of read operations. Furthermore, temporal pattern analysis was performed to observe how each file was accessed at each position. In addition, two different datasets were used, such as CIFAR and MNIST, in which the type of access is different; in CIFAR, the same file is shared for all processes, and with MNIST, the file is replicated per process. This behavior can have advantages and disadvantages, such as the need for synchronization, performance, and storage space. We hope to analyze other types of DL applications for future work to see their impact on file access patterns.

References

1. Pytorch. https://pytorch.org/docs/stable/index.html/. Accessed 24 Mar 2021
2. Abadi, M., et al.: TensorFlow: large-scale machine learning on heterogeneous systems (2015). https://www.tensorflow.org/, software available from tensorflow.org
3. Bae, M., Jeong, M., Yeo, S., Oh, S., Kwon, O.K.: I/O performance evaluation of large-scale deep learning on an HPC system. In: 2019 International Conference on High Performance Computing & Simulation (HPCS), pp. 436–439. IEEE (2019)
4. Brinkmann, A., et al.: Ad hoc file systems for high-performance computing. J. Comput. Sci. Technol. **35**(1), 4–26 (2020)
5. Byna, S., et al.: Exahdf5: delivering efficient parallel I/O on exascale computing systems. J. Comput. Sci. Technol. **35**(1), 145–160 (2020)
6. Carns, P., et al.: Understanding and improving computational science storage access through continuous characterization. Trans. Storage **7**(3), 8:1–8:26 (2011). https://doi.org/10.1145/2027066.2027068
7. Chollet, F., et al.: Keras. https://github.com/fchollet/keras (2015)
8. Dryden, N., Böhringer, R., Ben-Nun, T., Hoefler, T.: Clairvoyant prefetching for distributed machine learning I/O. In: Proceedings of the International Conference for High Performance Computing, Networking, Storage and Analysis. SC 2021, Association for Computing Machinery, New York (2021). https://doi.org/10.1145/3458817.3476181
9. Farhangi, A., Bian, J., Wang, J., Guo, Z.: Work-in-progress: a deep learning strategy for I/O scheduling in storage systems. In: 2019 IEEE Real-Time Systems Symposium (RTSS), pp. 568–571. IEEE (2019)
10. Jia, Y., et al.: Caffe: Convolutional architecture for fast feature embedding. arXiv preprint arXiv:1408.5093 (2014)
11. Krizhevsky, A.: Learning multiple layers of features from tiny images. Technical Report (2009)
12. LeCun, Y., Cortes, C., Burges, C.: MNIST. http://yann.lecun.com/exdb/mnist/. Accessed 24 Mar 2021
13. Mittal, S., Rajput, P., Subramoney, S.: A survey of deep learning on CPUs: opportunities and co-optimizations. IEEE Trans. Neural Netw. Learn. Syst. 1–21 (2021). https://doi.org/10.1109/TNNLS.2021.3071762
14. Paul, A.K., Karimi, A.M., Wang, F.: Characterizing machine learning I/O workloads on leadership scale HPC Systems. In: 2021 29th International Symposium on Modeling, Analysis, and Simulation of Computer and Telecommunication Systems (MASCOTS), pp. 1–8 (2021). https://doi.org/10.1109/MASCOTS53633.2021.9614303
15. Rojas, E., Kahira, A.N., Meneses, E., Gomez, L.B., Badia, R.M.: A study of checkpointing in large scale training of deep neural networks. arXiv preprint arXiv:2012.00825 (2020)
16. Sergeev, A., Balso, M.D.: Horovod: fast and easy distributed deep learning in TensorFlow. arXiv preprint arXiv:1802.05799 (2018)

17. Wan, L., et al.: I/O performance characterization and prediction through machine learning on hpc systems. In: CUG2020 Proceedings (2020)
18. Zacarias, F.V., Petrucci, V., Nishtala, R., Carpenter, P., Mossé, D.: Intelligent colocation of HPC workloads. J. Parall. Distrib. Comput. **151**, 125–137 (2021)
19. Zhang, Z., Huang, L., Pauloski, J.G., Foster, I.: Aggregating local storage for scalable deep learning I/O. In: 2019 IEEE/ACM Third Workshop on Deep Learning on Supercomputers (DLS), pp. 69–75. IEEE (2019)
20. Zhu, Y., et al.: Entropy-aware I/o pipelining for large-scale deep learning on HPC systems. In: 2018 IEEE 26th International Symposium on Modeling, Analysis, and Simulation of Computer and Telecommunication Systems (MASCOTS), pp. 145–156 (2018). https://doi.org/10.1109/MASCOTS.2018.00023
21. Zhu, Y., Yu, W., Jiao, B., Mohror, K., Moody, A., Chowdhury, F.: Efficient user-level storage disaggregation for deep learning. In: 2019 IEEE International Conference on Cluster Computing (CLUSTER), pp. 1–12 (2019). https://doi.org/10.1109/CLUSTER.2019.8891023
22. Zhu, Z., Tan, L., Li, Y., Ji, C.: PHDFS: optimizing I/O performance of HDFS in deep learning cloud computing platform. J. Syst. Archit. **109**, 101810 (2020)

A Survey on Billing Models
for Cloud-Native Applications

José Rodrigo Benítez Paredes[1(✉)] and Fabio López-Pires[1,2]

[1] Universidad Nacional de Asunción, San Lorenzo, Paraguay
rbenitez@pol.una.py
[2] Parque Tecnológico Itaipu, Foz do Iguaçu, Paraguay
fabio.lopez@pti.org.py
http://www.pol.una.py, https://www.pti.org.py

Abstract. Recent development in Cloud-Native Applications (CNAs) have stimulated the need to explore novel and applicable billing models. Cloud Service Providers (CSPs) are now beginning to include intervals more granular for pricing and resource allocation management strategie's, through an approach called *micro-billing*. Although many CSPs are applying billing techniques in sub-minute ranges, the existing specialized literature does not study *micro-billing* for CNAs and its correlation with *micro-services*. This work presents an exploratory research to identify main opportunities on billing models for CNAs through a systematic literature review to contribute as a basis for future research works in the field, mainly related to micro-billing models for CNAs.

Keywords: Cloud-Native Applications · Billing-models · Cloud billing · Micro-services · Micro-billing

1 Introduction

Problems related to cost analysis and billing for applications that are deployed on cloud computing infrastructure can be addressed with the existing billing models. In this context, it is essential the efficient use of cloud computing resources, especially, for software and hardware infrastructure (in hyper-scale environments), giving space to novel billing models as micro-billing.

An adequate and precise adoption of a micro-billing model could be an advantage for Cloud Service Providers (CSPs) and Cloud Service Consumers (CSCs), since this could allow them to improve the allocation of resources (economical revenue) and their corresponding billing (economical costs).

In this work, authors systematically explore the specialized literature in order to analyze existing billing models in cloud computing environments, focusing on the advantages of Cloud-Native Applications (CNAs). In [12], refers that the CSPs adjust the response capacity of the CNAs, adding or removing resources to respond to Quality of Service (QoS) requirements, facing provisioning variation, both for excess and deficit. With the characteristics of the CNAs, could take

© The Author(s), under exclusive license to Springer Nature Switzerland AG 2022
E. Rucci et al. (Eds.): JCC-BD&ET 2022, CCIS 1634, pp. 20–30, 2022.
https://doi.org/10.1007/978-3-031-14599-5_2

full advantage of rapid elasticity. This is extremely important for accurate and detailed micro-billing.

In this context, authors will provide a guide for research on the field, mainly considering that, to the best of the authors knowledge, there is no existing survey on this topic.

This work is structured in the following way: In Sect. 2, the process of selecting studied articles is indicated, showing a synthesis of the existing relevant literature and exploring billing models for cloud computing in general, and micro-billing in particular. In Sect. 3, main findings of the systematic literature review are presented, including topics considered as main factors of the studied billing strategies, results of the exploration and levels of incidence of the topics explored in the studied articles, as well as details on state-of-the-art reference models to encourage to explore and propose an extended theoretical model with improvements. Finally, in Sect. 4 conclusions and research opportunities are summarized.

2   Systematic Literature Review

A search and selection process has been carried out related to research work on billing models for cloud applications. This section presents a summary and analysis of the selected research works.

The process of selecting relevant articles began with a search for research articles in the Google Scholar Database [scholar.google.com]. It should be noted that the entire process of search was carried out in English, (1) the first search was carried out using the keyword: "Cloud Billing" obtaining a result of more than 999 articles from 2016 to 2021; then (2) it was narrowed using the title as search criteria, using at least the word: "Cloud Billing" from 2016 to 2021, whose result was 40 articles (3) the third search was narrowed by adding the keyword "Native" in reference to "Cloud-Native Applications", which resulted in 11 articles.

Given the large number of articles related to the first and second searches, a selection has been made based on the relevance of the topics, resulting in 15 articles selected that are presented in this section. In addition, for the selection criteria, was considered the mention or analysis of billing models for Cloud environments.

In [15], it is discussed how micro-billing and sub-second resource allocation can be considered in the context of streaming applications, and how micro-billing models pose challenges to cloud infrastructure management. The challenges include monitoring, analysis and action plans for subsequent deployment. It discusses how micro-billing can be important to face in practice. In addition, it is exposed that in this context, the rates of generation and arrival of data can be unpredictable and that the predictive analysis of the workload can minimize the overhead of resources, anticipating future demands.

In [3], several current and emerging challenges that must be overcome are analyzed and described, mainly on how billing platforms must be prepared to face these challenges, especially with the appearance of deployment models such as Fog and Edge and its relationship with Internet of Things (IoT) and Cloud Computing. Generic requirements for any accounting and billing solution dealing with heterogeneous services, data sources, among others are discussed. It presents some of the specific challenges that must be overcome to create a solution compatible with emerging technologies in cloud environments. In addition, the analysis of billing infrastructure requirements is presented in perspective depending on the requirement: if it is in real-time or not, or if you want billing to be pay-as-you-go, or if periodic billing in accounts would be enough, stating that all of the above could lead to the need for micro-billing in cloud environments. The study in [3] concludes that the analysis of costs and performance, based on the execution time of a proposed architecture, must be verified to evaluate the suitability of special needs such as micro-billing in the proposed scenarios. Furthermore an architecture in progress is proposed, which includes a micro-billing platform, which will be proposed in prototypes as future work.

In [11], aspects related to payment models and variables to be considered in Cloud Computing are addressed, focusing on the pay-as-you-go model. It describes a comparison of different payment methods of the Amazon Web Services (AWS) cloud service: Elastic Compute Cloud (EC2), summarized as follows:

- **On-Demand Instances:** Ideal option for occasional CSCs. You could increase or decrease the compute capacity, depending on the demand of your applications and pay only for the hours and instances used.
- **Reserved Instances:** Consider a billing model which allows applications with constant utilization and predictable workloads, to reserve instances in advance, allowing significant cost savings compared to On-Demand Instances, since it allows customers to deploy instances when necessary.
- **Dedicated Instances:** It consists in a Virtual Machine (VM) assigned to a specific client on a specific host.
- Dedicated Host: It is a Physical Machine (PM) inside an EC2 server, which is not shared by any other VM and the memory/CPU usage is not shared with anyone else.
- **Spot Instances:** This model can be applied to user applications, which have a flexible start and end as well as those that only require a very affordable price of computing capacity. The interruption of the service is acceptable or that require urgent and large amounts of extra capacity. In addition, the user can bid on compute services and bid maximums to deploy or stop services outside that threshold.

In [5], it is studied how to minimize the cost of the service in Edge Computing, guaranteeing the workload requirements. A combination between an Autoregressive Moving Average (ARIMA) model and a Back-Propagation (BP) Neural Network (NN) is designed and proposed to improve prediction accuracy, and then estimate in advance the load within the Edge Cloud Cluster. From the ARIMA model, the historical workload linear factor is extracted and then processed by the BP NN model and as a result of the combination of the predicted values of the two models, the final load prediction is obtained. With the premise of guaranteeing the Quality of Service (QoS) and minimizing the cost of the cluster, an adaptive resource allocation method for Edge Cloud Clusters is presented, which can reduce the cost of service considering the fine granularity of resource billing.

In [7], it is mentioned that the price of execution in cloud infrastructure depends on several aspects, they can be broadly classified as: *hard and soft factors*. Hard factors are fundamental differentiators and soft factors involve negotiable aspects between the client and the service provider. For example, the reliability of the service is a *hard factor*, that affects prices. Similarly, reserved and dedicated resources cost more than shared or on-demand resources. The *soft factors*, however, are flexible aspects of billing. They vary depending on aspects such as a company's association with a CSP, its purchasing power and opportunity factors. The CSP frequently auction their services at lower prices, so much that the CSP win in the auctions by limiting the time required in negotiations and sales negotiations and users get lower prices. In addition, [7] mention that is its needed to set limits on the usage of the infrastructure, known as *quotas*. Finally, the work on [7] proposes that architects must be thorough when validating the options at the beginning of a migration of an application, and some questions that are essential to choose the services of CSPs, including examples of questions to be asked about each of the proposed factors.

In [14], authors discusses how Tenant-Specific Virtual Switches allow cloud providers to amortize the costs of their virtual networks through detailed or granular billing and pricing by accounting for cycle times of CPUs used by Tenant-Specific Virtual Switches. In addition, IO and power can be taken into account. As it turns out, these mechanisms are particularly suitable for serverless architectures, where billing is naturally granular, i.e. per second rather than per hour or based on usage.

In [4], the architecture, operation, and implementation of monitoring and control applications developed in the *Secure Cloud Secure Big Data Processing* project on untrusted clouds is described within the context of the generation, transmission and distribution of electrical energy, which normally involves many operating losses. A scenario is proposed, where a meter probe receives a request from a Metering Data Collection (MDC) application, for its measurements accumulated in predefined periods. The period is configured in an application determined by the MDC, then cloud applications receive the data and store it in an encrypted database, using MySQL. The cloud application logs the consumption in a secure isolated region and sends only aggregated data to protect consumer privacy.

In [9], a model for billing in cloud for Platform as a Service (PaaS) and Software as a Service (SaaS) models was presented, based on an application of charges for use of resources (pay-as-you-go). The results obtained in [9] indicated that the use of billing models that allow billing based on the use of resources (pay-as-you-go) is a trend in Cloud Computing; where it was verified that the model proposed in the research was well accepted by users and administrators. However, it is mentioned that there are still (in some cases) managers who prefer to hire promotional packages. Although the work is quite complete, in terms of addressing billing models and variables used for this purpose within the platforms presented, it does not address issues related to micro-billing, nor micro-service architectures, essential for Cloud-Native Applications (CNAs).

In [10], the advantages of adopting alternative scheduling policies for the use of computational resources are analyzed, to take advantage of the inactive time intervals (idle) of the leased resources, both for the users, in terms of cost of service and for the CSPs, to correctly determine their operating costs. A real astronomy workflow application was used, configured by QoS parameters, with budgets and deadlines defined by the user, in addition to a set of programming algorithms that apply different policies, regarding the use of inactive VM instances, which executed different execution plans and resource provisioning. The results mentioned in [10], show that if they assume a policy of reusing the fractions already loaded from the last partially idle time intervals (idle); the cost of the service for the end user can be reduced and the competitiveness of providers increases by up to 21.6% in terms of operating costs. In addition, it is mentioned in the study that these fractions could be accessed by a user (non-owner), who would pay only for the fraction actually used, because the billing periods turn out to be long for many applications, which means that the leased resources are left inactive.

In [8], energy consumption and device billing costs are analyzed in the context of Internet of Things (IoT)-oriented services. A theoretical framework is proposed to establish trade-offs in energy consumption and billing costs of an IoT-oriented infrastructure, which include mobile devices that generate queries that are processed by a backend Cloud Computing service. The analysis includes energy consumption and billing rates for the cloud infrastructure. The system adapts resource consumption according to the volume of queries generated when switching between *active* and *inactive* states. In the study, experiments were performed with Beaglebone Linux embedded platforms and Amazon Web Services (AWS)-based backend processing, both for query generation, streaming, and similarity detection. In addition, it is shown that the model proposed in [8] forms a reference framework that accurately incorporates the effect of the application of various system parameters with respect to energy consumption and billing costs in cloud environments.

In [2], a detailed study is carried out on the problem of the *under or over* use of resources in cloud infrastructures, and how clients do not have precise information regarding the billing mechanisms applied at their services. It becomes clear that, in many cases, CSPs cannot cope with the high demand and usage peaks of their clients' services in their infrastructures, therefore, they need to redirect these services to another cloud infrastructure in a cloud federation, and thus respond to the demands of its customers. However, this model brings with it many benefits, but also many associated problems, which are described in the work. However, the study is addressed in a special way, on accounting and billing, from the CSPs to the CSCs and between CSPs. Although in [2] it makes special mention that at present, it is necessary to address with greater emphasis the study of a reference framework for billing within the cloud federations, since in itself, it is a emerging field in research topics, does not differentiate on the types of services, such as web applications or Cloud-Native Applications, deployed in infrastructures, which are intended to be addressed in the present survey.

In [13] a billing model for cloud services is proposed, although there is no specific mention of the types of services to be billed, an approach is made on calculations regarding CPU usage, Memory, Disk (Read & Write) and Network Traffic. An information-capture model based on a load distribution mechanism in N nodes within the cloud server is proposed. The collection of consumption is carried out in each one of the nodes, and is registered in the Billing Server for its calculation. Since the hardware characteristics can be different in each node, the price is also different, so they are calculated independently for each node. The study presents precision results in the measurement of the CPU, Memory, Hardware (Read and Write), and Network (Read and Write) components, close to 95%, quite high and important indicators, moreover, even distant for billing calculation needs in cloud environments.

In [1], it is mentioned that currently available billing systems for cloud environments are limited in terms of computing load verification; which, does not allow the end user to verify the consumption records and, if they are correct or not, therefore: the model Verification & Approval Management System (VAMS) is proposed, which aims to provide a dynamic mechanism billing verification for cloud users and CSPs. In addition, according to [1], the proposed model provides security to access cloud resources and manage data access control. The main concept is to verify the computational resources consumed by a cloud user in a neutral way and without any possibility of intervention between users and CSPs directly, since all resource billing is managed by the VAMS model.

In [6], a secure data storage and processing model in the cloud has been proposed, designed and implemented, which can preserve the privacy of the user and the confidentiality of the data obtained from the intelligent electricity meters consumption. The model uses a Homomorphic Asymmetric Key Cryptosystem (HAKC) to encrypt data, which allows most of the billing calculation work to be carried out in the cloud, based on the aggregation of encrypted readings from the smart meters. The experiments of the work show several factors that can influence the homomorphic calculation time in the cloud, such as the duration of a billing period, the number of smart meters involved in the measurement, even by the number of operations of homomorphic sums.

In [16], the monitoring and billing modules based on Docklet, which is a lightweight cloud-based system deployed in a Linux container, is presented. A monitoring and *micro-billing* or granular billing method is proposed to improve the Docklet System. Experiments in [16], showed that the proposed method is efficient and has a low workload on the system. Docklet records charges to be billed to users based on how much resources they have used. The billing rules are given by:

- Time the container has been running, based on a Time.
- Billing upload stops, if a container stop operation is launched, while if it is removed, uploading will be done by the hour, no matter how much it has consumed since the last upload.
- When users' credits drop to zero, all running user clusters will stop and users will not be able to create, start, or scale out any clusters until their credits are more than zero.

3   Main Findings and Discussion

Table 1. Variables addressed in the different articles analyzed.

Topics	Articles	[1]	[2]	[3]	[4]	[5]	[6]	[7]	[8]	[9]	[10]	[11]	[13]	[14]	[15]	[16]
Micro-services	Analyzes	–	–	✓	–	–	–	✓	–	–	–	–	–	–	–	–
	Proposes	–	–	✓	–	–	–	✓	–	–	–	–	–	–	–	–
Micro-Billing	Analyzes	–	–	✓	–	–	–	✓	–	–	–	–	–	–	✓	–
	Proposes	–	–	✓	–	–	–	–	–	–	–	–	–	–	–	–
Cloud-Billing	Analyzes	✓	✓	✓	✓	✓	–	✓	✓	✓	✓	✓	✓	✓	✓	✓
	Proposes	–	–	✓	–	–	–	–	✓	✓	✓	–	✓	–	–	✓
Billing-models	Analyzes	✓	✓	✓	–	✓	✓	–	✓	✓	✓	✓	✓	–	✓	✓
	Proposes	✓	–	✓	–	✓	✓	–	✓	✓	✓	–	✓	–	–	✓
Pay-as-you-go	Analyzes	✓	–	✓	–	–	–	✓	–	✓	✓	✓	✓	–	✓	–
	Proposes	–	–	✓	–	–	–	–	–	✓	–	–	✓	–	–	–
Subscription	Analyzes	–	–	–	–	–	–	✓	–	–	–	–	✓	–	–	–
	Proposes	–	–	–	–	–	–	–	–	–	–	–	–	–	–	–
Cloud-Native	Analyzes	–	–	–	✓	–	–	✓	–	✓	–	–	–	–	–	–
	Proposes	–	–	–	–	–	–	–	–	✓	–	–	–	–	–	–

Based on the studied articles, this sections presents the main findings of this survey, referring to billing models in cloud computing in general, with special attention and discussion on micro-billing for CNAs.

As a summary of the studied works, Table 1 presents main topics addressed in the specialized literature with a detail on which of the studied articles *Analyzes* and/or *Proposes* each of the presented topics. Additionally, Fig. 1 shows the percentage of studied articles and addressed each of the considered topics.

The main identified findings are listed as follows:

- **Main Finding 1:** Only 3 articles, **20%**, [4,7,9] mention CNAs concepts, and only one of them propose a billing model for CNAs [9].
- **Main Finding 2:** Only **20%** [3,7,15], analyze, mention or discuss micro-billing related topics, and even more, only one **6.7%** of them proposes a prototype oriented to micro-billing [15].
- **Main Finding 3:** Only **13.3%** analyze aspects of Micro-services [3,7], and of those, only one, [7], proposes some operating scheme through Micro-services or simply mentions it.

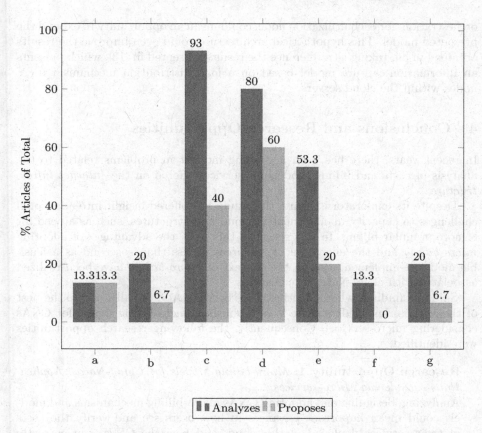

Fig. 1. Level of approach to topics in reviewed articles - Ref: a: Micro-services, b: Micro-billing, c: Cloud-Billing, d: Billing-models, e: Pay-as-you-go, f: Subscription, g: Cloud-Native

- **Main Finding 4:** 93,3% of the Articles studied mention or discuss Cloud Billing related topics, but only 40% propose a Cloud Billing model.
- **Main Finding 5:** 80% of the referred Articles analyze, in general, topics related to billing models, and of these, 60% proposes some billing models.
- **Main Finding 6:** 10 of 15 Articles studied, that represents **66.6%** of the total, **do not mention** any topics related to Micro-services, micro-billing and CNAs, although 9 of those 11 do mention billing models.

Based on the main findings of this study, there are opportunities for exploration to deepen the studies carried out in [3,7,9,13,15] which would allow the adopt of micro-billing models for CNAs, which, according to the results of this study, are not being specifically addressed in the technical literature.

Although the work of [9], presents a model for billing in cloud for Platform as a Service (PaaS) and Software as a Service (SaaS) models, the use of containers or micro -services, is not explicitly mentioned. The adoption of Micro-services orchestration, for each utilization node, could mean an opportunity to expand the presented model. This hypothetical architecture could even improve the results obtained in [9], taking as a reference the results presented in [13], which presents an information-capture model based on a load distribution mechanism in N nodes within the cloud servers.

4 Conclusions and Research Opportunities

In recent years, there has been a growing interest in problems related to the analysis of costs and billing models for services offered on the *Internet infrastructure*.

Despite its exploratory nature, this study has offered insight into additional challenges to capacity management in cloud infrastructures, such as a need for a more granular billing. In this sense, in this work the advantages of adopting *micro-billing* and the allocation of resources in less than a second as a feasible model of implementation in the context of *micro-billing* have been realized associated with cloud-Native applications.

Six main findings where identified (See Sect. 3). Additionally, and to the best of the authors knowledge, there is no published micro-billing model for CNAs considering micro-services. Consequently, the following research opportunities were identified.

– **Research Opportunity 1:** *Micro-billing Models for Cloud-Native Applications considering Micro-services.*
  Analyzing, designing and adopting CNAs micro-billing mechanisms and models could mean important advances in how users see and verify the costs of their services deployed in the cloud, and how the CSPs, can correctly determine their operating costs. This is a topic that has not been formally addressed in the studied technical literature.
– **Research Opportunity 2:** *Distributed CNAs micro-milling Schemes for Cloud Federations.*
  In the peaks of demand for services, assuring the SLAs established, the CSPs are forced to redirect the services to other CSPs, known as a Cloud Federation. One of the main challenges is how to manage the distributed billing of each service provided by each CSP. The adoption of Distributed CNAs micro-billing schemes for Cloud Federations, could provide important benefits, for the users and for each of CSP, members of the Cloud Federation.
– **Research Opportunity 3:** *Micro-billing Schemes for Showback in Private Corporate Cloud.*
  In private clouds it is crucial to know the total operating costs invested in IT. Although they are not billed to internal users, it is important to define micro-billing schemes for CNAs, and account for the use of resources for their return under Showback schemes.
– **Research Opportunity 4:** *Smart allocation for distributed Cloud-Native Applications.*

As mentioned in Research Opportunity 2, the management of micro-billing in federated cloud environments is vital, in addition to this, ensuring the optimal selection and execution of redirected services availables in other federated CSPs, generates the challenge of finding mechanisms for smart selection and location of CNAs services, according to multi-objective criteria.

References

1. Biswas, H., Sarddar, D.: Verification as a Service (VaaS): a trusted multipurpose service for accounting, billing verification and approval of consumed resources at low computational overhead to enhance the cloud usability. Int. J. Appl. Eng. Res. **13**, 14402–14410 (2018). ISSN 0973-4562
2. Dhuria, S., Gupta, A., Singla, R.K.: Accounting and billing of physical resources in cloud federation: a review. Int. J. Adv. Res. Comput. Sci. **9**(1), 834–841 (2018)
3. Harsh, P., Serhiienko, O.: Accounting and billing challenges in large scale emerging cloud technologies. In: CLOSER, pp. 390–399 (2020)
4. Joint EU-Brazil Research and Innovation Action: Cloud-native applications for billing, fraud detection, energy balance, energy delivering and fault detectioin D5. 2. Joint EU-Brazil Research and Innovation Action 1 (2017)
5. Li, C., et al.: Adaptive resource allocation based on the billing granularity in edge-cloud architecture. Comput. Commun. **145** (2019). ISSN: 0140-3664. https://doi.org/10.1016/j.comcom.2019.05.014. https://www.sciencedirect.com/science/article/pii/S0140366418310673
6. Mai, V., Khalil, I.: Design and implementation of a secure cloud-based billing model for smart meters as an Internet of things using homomorphic cryptography. Futur. Gener. Comput. Syst. **72**, 327–338 (2017)
7. Rajasekharaiah, C.: Cloud-Based Microservices: Techniques Challenges, and Solutions. Apress, Berkeley (2021). ISBN: 978-1-4842-6564-2. https://doi.org/10.1007/978-1-4842-6564-2_7
8. Renna, F., et al.: Media query processing for the Internet-of-Things: coupling of device energy consumption and cloud infrastructure billing. IEEE Trans. Multimedia **18**(12), 2537–2552 (2016)
9. Ribas, M., et al.: A platform as a service billing model for cloud computing management approaches. IEEE Lat. Am. Trans. **14**(1), 267–280 (2016)
10. Silva Sampaio, A.M., Barbosa, J.G.: A study on cloud cost efficiency by exploiting idle billing period fractions. In: 2016 IEEE International Conference on Cloud Engineering Workshop (IC2EW), pp. 138–143. IEEE (2016)
11. Sehgal, N.K., Bhatt, P.C.P., Acken, J.M.: Cost and billing practices in cloud. In: Cloud Computing with Security: Concepts and Practices, pp. 173–191. Springer, Cham (2020). https://doi.org/10.1007/978-3-030-24612-9_10. ISBN: 978-3-030-24612-9
12. Spillner, J., et al.: Co-transformation to cloud-native applications: development experiences and experimental evaluation. In: 8th International Conference on Cloud Computing and Services Science (CLOSER), Funchal, Portugal, 19–21 March 2018. SciTePress (2018)
13. Sui, B., et al.: Billing system design of cloud services. In: 2018 3rd International Conference on Control, Automation and Artificial Intelligence (CAAI 2018). Atlantis Press (2018)

14. Thimmaraju, K., Schmid, S.: Towards fine-grained billing for cloud networking. arXiv preprint arXiv:2003.10745 (2020)
15. Tolosana-Calasanz, R., et al.: Capacity management for streaming applications over cloud infrastructures with micro billing models. In: Proceedings of the 9th International Conference on Utility and Cloud Computing, pp. 251–256 (2016)
16. Zhu, Y., et al.: Monitoring and billing of a lightweight cloud system based on Linux container. In: 2017 IEEE 37th International Conference on Distributed Computing Systems Workshops (ICDCSW), pp. 325–329. IEEE (2017)

Performance Analysis of AES on CPU-GPU Heterogeneous Systems

Victoria Sanz[1,2]([✉]), Adrián Pousa[1], Marcelo Naiouf[1], and Armando De Giusti[1,3]

[1] III-LIDI, School of Computer Sciences, National University of La Plata,
La Plata, Argentina
[2] CIC, Buenos Aires, Argentina
[3] CONICET, Buenos Aires, Argentina
{vsanz,apousa,mnaiouf,degiusti}@lidi.info.unlp.edu.ar

Abstract. AES is one of the most widely used encryption algorithms. With the ever-increasing amount of sensitive data that need protection, it is natural to turn to parallel AES solutions that exploit emerging architectures and reduce encryption time. In this paper, we present a collaborative implementation of AES (PAES-CPU-MultiGPU) for CPU-GPU heterogeneous systems. PAES-CPU-MultiGPU takes advantage of the hardware support for AES provided by modern CPU cores and, at the same time, benefits from the GPUs available on these systems. We compare the performance of our proposal with that of two other solutions that use only the CPU cores (PAES-CPU) and only the GPUs of the system (PAES-MultiGPU). The results reveal that PAES-CPU-MultiGPU achieves an overall performance similar to that of PAES-CPU, but using fewer CPU cores, outperforming by far PAES-MultiGPU. Also, PAES-CPU-MultiGPU outperforms PAES-CPU when an amount of CPU cores similar to that of commodity multicore machines is used.

Keywords: Advanced Encryption Standard · Data protection · CPU-GPU Heterogeneous Systems · CPU-GPU Collaborative Computing · Hybrid programming

1 Introduction

Nowadays, the amount of sensitive data that is generated to be stored and/or transmitted over the network is constantly increasing. To protect sensitive data from potential threats, encryption strategies are used. AES (Advanced Encryption Standard) [1] is one of the most widely used encryption algorithms and is considered secure enough to protect national information by the United States government [2].

Several libraries implement AES in software, being OpenSSL [3] one of the most used. Also, different processors (Intel, AMD, ARM) provide an instruction set to accelerate AES in hardware [4–6].

© The Author(s), under exclusive license to Springer Nature Switzerland AG 2022
E. Rucci et al. (Eds.): JCC-BD&ET 2022, CCIS 1634, pp. 31–42, 2022.
https://doi.org/10.1007/978-3-031-14599-5_3

The time involved in data encryption is directly related to the amount of data to be encrypted and may be significant. Several works have focused on reducing this time in AES, by taking advantage of emerging parallel architectures such as GPUs and multicore CPUs [7–13].

In general, GPUs have proven to be more efficient than multicore CPUs when encrypting data using AES implemented in software. However, encryption on multicore CPUs with hardware support for AES has proven more efficient than encryption on GPUs, when enough CPU cores are used. Even so, GPUs are a good option compared to CPUs with few cores and, also, have the advantage of not requiring specific hardware support [12, 13].

Although modern computers include multiple CPU cores and at least one GPU, little work has been done to accelerate AES on such systems, i.e. by benefiting from both types of processing units. In [14] the authors present a file protecting system that uses SHA3 and parallel software-based AES. They conclude that the hybrid version for heterogeneous systems with few CPU cores and a single GPU outperforms the GPU-only and CPU-only parallel versions.

In this paper, we present a collaborative implementation of AES (PAES-CPU-MultiGPU) for CPU-GPU heterogeneous systems. PAES-CPU-MultiGPU takes advantage of the hardware support for AES provided by modern CPU cores and, at the same time, benefits from the GPUs available on these systems. We compare the performance of our proposal with that of two other solutions that use only the CPU cores (PAES-CPU) and only the GPUs of the system (PAES-MultiGPU). The results reveal that PAES-CPU-MultiGPU achieves an overall performance similar to that of PAES-CPU, but using fewer CPU cores, outperforming by far PAES-MultiGPU. Also, PAES-CPU-MultiGPU outperforms PAES-CPU when an amount of CPU cores similar to that of commodity multicore machines is used (4, 6, 8 and 12 cores).

Our work differs from [14] in several ways. Our algorithm uses hardware-based AES on CPU cores and hides data transfer latency between CPU and GPU, leading to higher throughput. Also, our analysis is carried out on architectures that include more computing resources (up to 36 CPU cores and 2 GPUs) and with larger input data (2 GB to 32 GB).

The rest of the paper is organized as follows. Section 2 summarizes the AES algorithm, the architectural characteristics of heterogeneous systems and some related work. Section 3 overviews the parallel implementations of AES developed in our previous work. Section 4 presents our collaborative implementation of AES (PAES-CPU-MultiGPU). Section 5 shows our experimental results. Finally, Sect. 6 presents the main conclusions and future research.

2   Background

This section provides background information on the AES algorithm, the architectural characteristics of heterogeneous systems, and reviews related work.

2.1   AES Algorithm

The AES (Advanced Encryption Standard) algorithm [1] divides the input data into fixed-size blocks (128 bits). Each block is represented as a 4×4 matrix of bytes, called *state* (Fig. 1). The algorithm described in the standard applies eleven *rounds* to each state, where each round is composed of a set of operations.

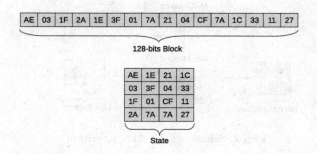

Fig. 1. AES state

Since AES is a symmetric algorithm, it uses the same key (*initial key*) to encrypt and decrypt the data. The key size is 128 bits, as indicated by the standard. From this key, ten more keys are generated through a mathematical procedure. The resulting keys (eleven in total) are called *sub-keys* and they are used one in each of the rounds.

Figure 2 shows the algorithm scheme. The encryption process starts with the *initial round*. This round performs only the *AddRoundKey* operation, which combines each byte of the state with the corresponding byte of the *initial key* using bitwise XOR. Each of the following nine rounds (*standard rounds*) applies 4 operations in this order:

- *SubBytes:* each state byte is replaced by another one. The new byte is taken from a 16×16 table (called Byte Substitution Table or S-box) that stores pre-computed values. This table is accessed taking the first 4 bits of the byte to be replaced as the row index and the last 4 bits as column index.
- *ShiftRows:* each row of the state is cyclically shifted to the left. Specifically, the ith row is shifted i times ($0 \leq i \leq 3$).
- *MixColumns:* a linear transformation is applied to each column of the state.
- *AddRoundKey:* this is the same as the initial round, but using the following subkey.

The *final round* performs 3 operations, *SubBytes*, *ShiftRows* and *AddRound-Key*, which work in the same way as in standard rounds. In this case, the *AddRoundKey* operation uses the last subkey.

The decryption process applies the same procedure but in reverse order.

Other variants of the standard consider 192 or 256-bits keys and require increasing the number of rounds and consequently generating more sub-keys.

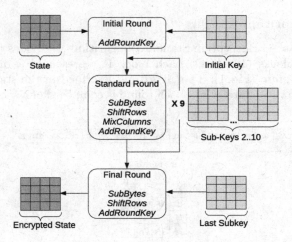

Fig. 2. Scheme of the AES algorithm

In this paper, we focus on evaluating the AES algorithm defined in the standard, which considers 128-bits keys, and only the encryption process, since decryption has similar performance.

2.2 Characterization of Heterogeneous Systems

Today, many of the systems used in High Performance Computing are heterogeneous systems that include general-purpose processors (multicore CPUs) and co-processors (typically GPUs). This trend is reflected in the Top500 [15] and Green500 [16] ranks, which list the most powerful computers and the most energy-efficient supercomputers in the world, respectively.

On the one hand, current multicore processors include tens of CPU cores on the same chip. Furthermore, a machine may include several of these processors, thus increasing the total number of cores.

On the other hand, a GPU (*device*) is a coprocessor that is connected to a conventional CPU (*host*) via PCIe. Computing on a GPU implies transferring data from CPU memory to GPU memory (*host-to-device* transfer, aka H2D) and viceversa (*device-to-host* transfer, aka D2H).

In general, an NVIDIA GPU is composed of several multiprocessors, called Streaming Multiprocessors (SMs). Each SM has multiple CUDA cores, load/store units for memory operations and special function units (SFUs). Also, GPUs have a multi-level memory hierarchy, whose components differ in size and access latency: global memory (high latency), constant memory (medium latency) and a shared memory in each SM (low latency).

Programming a CPU-GPU heterogeneous system requires using extensions to C Language such as Pthreads or OpenMP, for managing the CPU cores, and OpenCL or CUDA, for managing the GPUs.

2.3   Related Work

So far, different studies were performed on the acceleration of AES using parallel architectures. This section summarizes the most representative ones.

On the one hand, several researchers have analyzed software-based AES solutions on different parallel architectures. In particular, different authors [7–10] parallelized AES on NVIDIA GPUs, achieving higher performance than the sequential version provided by OpenSSL. Other authors [11,12] compared the performance of AES on NVIDIA GPUs and multicore CPUs with 8 threads, for input data less than 256 MB, and conclude that the GPU performs best.

On the other hand, several studies have assessed hardware-based AES solutions. Specifically, in [17] the authors compared a sequential AES solution, implemented using Intel AES New Instructions (AES-NI) [4], and AES on an NVIDIA GPU. The results indicate that the former achieves better performance and, also, they both improve the sequential software-based AES solution.

Moreover, in [12] the authors ran AES-NI on a multicore with up to 8 threads, for data less than 256 MB, and compared it against AES on a best-performing NVIDIA GPU. The results show that AES on this GPU outperforms sequential AES-NI. However, AES-NI with 4 threads is 1.4 times faster than AES on GPU.

Furthermore, in [13] we compared the performance of a hardware-based AES solution for multicore CPU with that of two other software-based AES solutions for multicore CPU and GPU respectively. The former is implemented using AES-NI and the latter using OpenSSL. The results reveal that the parallel hardware-based solution for CPU achieves higher performance. However, the solution for GPU (on 2 GPUs) is competitive compared to CPUs with hardware support for AES and few cores and CPUs that do not support AES.

Finally, in [14] the authors presented a highly efficient file protecting system that uses SHA3 (Secure Hash Algorithm 3) and parallel software-based AES. In particular, they explored three variants adopting CPU, GPU and CPU+GPU parallelism respectively. They found that the hybrid variant outperforms the GPU-only variant, and both outperform the CPU-only variant.

3   Previous Implementations of AES

This section overviews the parallel implementations of AES developed in our previous work [13]. Specifically, AES for multicore CPU (PAES-CPU) and AES for single-GPU (PAES-GPU) and multi-GPU (PAES-MultiGPU).

3.1   AES for Multicore CPU

PAES-CPU uses OpenMP to manage multiple threads. This solution considers the input data as consecutive states (16 bytes). Each thread takes a proportional set of successive states from the input and applies the encryption process to each state. Each state is encrypted using the hardware support for AES provided by our Intel-based machine: the AES New Instructions (AES-NI) [4].

Specifically, AES-NI consists of six instructions: four instructions for encryption/decryption and two for generating sub-keys. Table 1 shows these six instructions and their functionality.

Table 1. AES new instructions

Instruction	Description
AESENC	Performs one standard round of AES encryption
AESENCLAST	Performs the final round of AES encryption
AESDEC	Performs one standard round of AES decryption
AESDECLAST	Performs the final round of AES decryption
AESKEYGENASSIST	Generates the sub-keys used for encryption
AESIMC	Performs the Inverse MixColumns Transformation, in order to convert the encryption sub-keys to a Form usable for decryption

3.2   AES for Single-GPU and Multi-GPU

PAES-GPU is developed using CUDA and performs the following steps. First, the host copies the subkeys and the Byte Substitution Table into the constant memory of the GPU, since they are read-only. Then, it copies the data to be encrypted into the global memory of the device (*H2D* transfer) and launches the kernel.

Similar to PAES-CPU, PAES-GPU considers the input data as consecutive states. The threads belonging to the same CUDA block work on successive states. For that purpose, they cooperate to efficiently load the states to be encrypted into shared memory. Then, each thread is responsible for encrypting one state. In this case, the state is encrypted using the OpenSSL `AES_encrypt` function that we adapted for GPUs. After that, the threads cooperate to move the encrypted data from shared memory to global memory.

Finally, the host gets the encrypted data from the global memory of the GPU (*D2H* transfer).

Note that GPUs have limited memory capacity. Therefore, when the workload exceeds this capacity, it is divided into chunks that fit into global memory, and then they are transfered and encrypted one by one.

Also, it should be noted that *H2D/D2H* transfers are time-consuming, since they involve PCIe communication. To hide this latency, PAES-GPU uses CUDA *streams* [18] to overlap communication and computation.

PAES-MultiGPU considers a system with several identical GPUs, hence the workload (input data) is distributed equally among them. In this case, PAES-MultiGPU creates as many threads as available GPUs (using OpenMP). Each thread runs on a dedicated CPU core and controls one GPU.

4   AES for CPU-GPU Heterogeneous Systems

Our collaborative implementation of AES (PAES-CPU-MultiGPU) is developed using OpenMP and CUDA. Assuming a system composed of N CPU cores and M GPUs, PAES-CPU-MultiGPU creates two sets of threads. The first set has M threads, each one runs on a dedicated CPU core and controls one GPU. The second set has $N - M$ threads, which execute concurrently on the remaining CPU cores.

PAES-CPU-MultiGPU also considers the input data as consecutive states. This workload is distributed between the CPU cores and the GPUs so that these processing units complete their respective work within the same amount of time.

Specifically, the distribution strategy is based on the relative performance of the processing units [19] and requires calculating R, i.e. the proportion of work assigned to the CPU cores. R is given by $\frac{T_{gpu}}{T_{cpu}+T_{gpu}}$, where T_{cpu} represents the execution time of the OpenMP algorithm on the available CPU cores and T_{gpu} is the execution time of the single-GPU or multi-GPU algorithm, as appropriate. R arises from supposing that the execution time of the collaborative implementation reaches its minimum when $T_{cpu} \cdot R = T_{gpu} \cdot (1 - R)$. According to R, the workload assigned to the CPU cores is $D_{cpu} = R \cdot D_{size}$ and the workload assigned to the GPU(s) is $D_{gpu} = D_{size} - D_{cpu}$, where D_{size} is the number of states.

Once the workload was distributed, PAES-CPU (Sect. 3.1) is used to encrypt the states on the CPU cores, while PAES-MultiGPU is used to encrypt the states on the GPUs (Sect. 3.2).

Figure 3 illustrates PAES-CPU-MultiGPU.

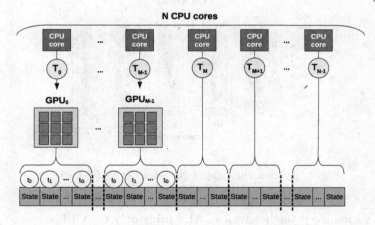

Fig. 3. Scheme of PAES-CPU-MultiGPU

5   Experimental Results

Our experimental platform is a machine composed of two Intel Xeon E5-2695 v4 processors and 128 GB RAM. Each processor has eighteen 2.10 Ghz cores, thus the machine has thirty-six cores in total. Hyper-Threading and Turbo Boost were disabled. The machine is equipped with two Nvidia GeForce GTX 960; each one is composed of 1024 cores and 2 GB GDDR5 memory. Each CUDA core operates at 1127 Mhz.

Tests were performed using data of different sizes (2 GB, 4 GB, 8 GB, 16 GB and 32 GB) and focusing on the encryption process, since the decryption process has a similar performance.

To evaluate the effectiveness of our proposal, we executed the following parallel implementations of AES: AES for multicore CPU (PAES-CPU), AES for single-GPU (PAES-GPU), AES for multi-GPU (PAES-MultiGPU) and AES for general CPU-GPU heterogeneous systems (PAES-CPU-MultiGPU).

PAES-CPU and PAES-CPU-MultiGPU were executed with the following system configurations: 6, 12, 18, 24, 30 and 36 threads/CPU cores.

The implementations of AES that use GPUs were executed with 256 threads per *CUDA block* and 32 *CUDA streams*. We experimentally determined that the best performance is achieved using these values. Also, our analysis considers the data transfer time (*H2D/D2H* transfers), since it represents a significant portion of the total execution time (i.e. it is not negligible).

For each test scenario (input and system configuration), we ran each solution 100 times and averaged the Gbps.

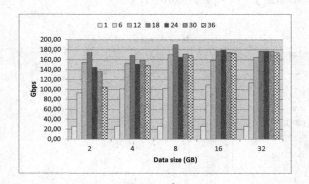

Fig. 4. Average throughput (in Gbps) of PAES-CPU

First, we analyzed the behavior of AES using only the CPU cores.

Figure 4 illustrates the throughput (in Gbps) achieved by PAES-CPU, for different data sizes and system configurations (number of threads/ cores). In general, it is observed that the best performance is reached with 18 threads/cores, regardless of the data size. Adding more threads/cores does not bring significant performance gains. In summary, the sequential solution (1 thread/core) reaches an average throughput of 26.04 Gbps, while the parallel solution with 18 threads/cores obtains an average throughput of 177.66 Gbps and a peak throughput of 190.13 Gbps with 8 GB data.

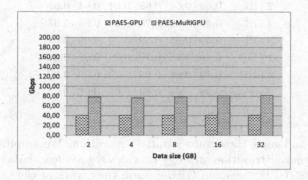

Fig. 5. Average throughput (in Gbps) of PAES-GPU and PAES-MultiGPU

Next, we evaluated the behavior of AES on GPUs.

Figure 5 shows the throughput (in Gbps) of PAES-GPU and PAES-MultiGPU, for different data sizes. To sum up, the solution with 1 GPU (PAES-GPU) reaches an average throughput of 40.69 Gbps, while the solution with 2 GPUs (PAES-MultiGPU) obtains an average throughput of 79.23 Gbps.

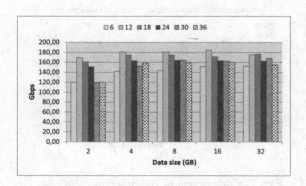

Fig. 6. Average throughput (in Gbps) of PAES-CPU-MultiGPU

Then, we studied the behavior of AES using CPUs and GPUs together.

For that purpose, we distributed the input data among the CPU cores and the GPUs according to the strategy proposed in Sect. 4. Table 2 shows the value of R calculated for each input size and number of CPU cores. From the table we can see that the value of R does not vary significantly with the size of the input. For this reason, we calculated the average value of R for each number

Table 2. Values of R used by PAES-CPU-MultiGPU

	No. of CPU cores					
	6	12	18	24	30	36
2 GB	0.46	0.64	0.68	0.64	0.64	0.61
4 GB	0.49	0.66	0.70	0.67	0.65	0.67
8 GB	0.49	0.65	0.69	0.70	0.69	0.68
16 GB	0.49	0.66	0.70	0.69	0.68	0.68
32 GB	0.49	0.66	0.69	0.69	0.69	0.68
Average	0.48	0.65	0.69	0.68	0.67	0.67

of CPU cores and used these values during execution. We empirically proved that our workload distribution strategy provides a good load-balance, since the processing units (CPU cores and GPUs) finish their work at the same time.

Figure 6 presents the throughput (in Gbps) achieved by PAES-CPU-MultiGPU, for different data sizes and system configurations (number of threads/cores). In general, it is observed that the best performance is reached with 12 threads /cores. Similarly to PAES-CPU, adding more threads/cores does not bring significant performance gains. In particular, PAES-CPU-MultiGPU with 12 threads /cores obtains an average throughput of 178.04 Gbps and a peak throughput of 184.26 Gbps with 16 GB data.

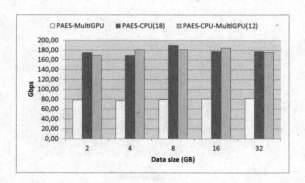

Fig. 7. Comparison of the different solutions

Figure 7 compares the throughput (in Gbps) of the algorithms. In the case of PAES-CPU and PAES-CPU-MultiGPU, we selected the system configuration that provides the best performance in general. The results reveal that PAES-CPU-MultiGPU with 12 CPU cores and PAES-CPU with 18 CPU cores obtain a similar performance, which significantly exceeds that of PAES-MultiGPU. Note that PAES-CPU-MultiGPU reaches its best performance using fewer CPU cores than PAES-CPU.

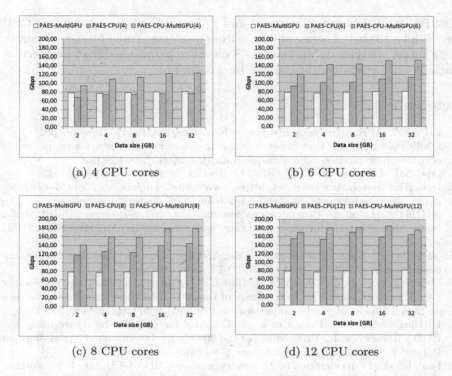

(a) 4 CPU cores

(b) 6 CPU cores

(c) 8 CPU cores

(d) 12 CPU cores

Fig. 8. Comparison of the different solutions on commodity multicore machines

Finally, we compare the performance of PAES-CPU and PAES-CPU-MultiGPU when using an amount of CPU cores similar to that of commodity multicore machines (4, 6, 8 and 12 cores). Furthermore, these solutions were contrasted with the one that uses only the GPUs (PAES-MultiGPU). Figure 8 shows the throughput obtained (in Gbps). From the results we can deduce that on machines with few cores (at most 12), using the CPU cores and the GPUs collaboratively improves performance compared to using only the CPU cores or only the GPUs of the system.

6 Conclusions and Future Work

In this paper, we presented an implementation of AES for CPU-GPU heterogeneous systems, which uses both CPU cores and GPUs for encryption.

We compared the performance of our proposal (PAES-CPU-MultiGPU) with that of two other solutions that use only the CPU cores (PAES-CPU) and only the GPUs of the system (PAES-MultiGPU).

From the analysis we conclude that PAES-CPU-MultiGPU achieves an overall performance (178.04 Gbps) similar to that of PAES-CPU (177.66 Gbps), but using fewer CPU cores, outperforming by far PAES-MultiGPU (79.23 Gbps).

Also, PAES-CPU-MultiGPU outperforms PAES-CPU when an amount of CPU cores similar to that of commodity multicore machines is used (4, 6, 8, 12 cores).

In future, we plan to evaluate AES on other parallel architectures such as Single Board Computers (SBCs) and Intel Xeon Phi.

References

1. FIPS 197: AES. http://csrc.nist.gov/publications/fips/fips197/fips-197.pdf
2. CNSS Policy No. 15, Fact Sheet No. 1. http://csrc.nist.gov/csrc/media/projects/cryptographic-module-validation-program/documents/cnss15fs.pdf
3. OpenSSL: Cryptography and SSL/TLS Toolkit. https://www.openssl.org
4. Intel AES New Instructions Set. https://www.intel.com/content/dam/doc/white-paper/advanced-encryption-standard-new-instructions-set-paper.pdf
5. AMD64 Architecture Programmer's Manual, Vol. 4: 128-Bit and 256-Bit Media Instructions. http://developer.amd.com/wordpress/media/2012/10/26568_APM_v41.pdf
6. ARM Armv8-A A32/T32 Instruction Set Architecture. http://developer.arm.com/documentation/ddi0597/2021-06/SIMD-FP-Instructions
7. Manavski, S. A. et al.: CUDA compatible GPU as an efficient hardware accelerator for AES cryptography. In: Proceedings of the 2007 IEEE International Conference on Signal Processing and Communications (ICSPC 2007), pp. 65–68 (2007)
8. Di Biagio, A. et al.: Design of a parallel AES for graphics hardware using the CUDA framework. In: Proceedings of the 2009 IEEE International Symposium on Parallel & Distributed Processing, pp. 1–8 (2009)
9. Iwai, K., et al.: Acceleration of AES encryption on CUDA GPU. Int. J. Networking Comput. **2**(1), 131–145 (2012)
10. Pousa, A., et al.: Performance analysis of a symmetric cryptographic algorithm on multicore architectures. In: Computer Science & Technology Series. XVII Argentine Congress of Computer Science Selected Papers, pp. 57–66. EDULP, Argentina (2012)
11. Ortega, J. et al.: Parallelizing AES on multicores and GPUs. In: Proceedings of the 2011 IEEE International Conference on Electro/Information Technology, pp. 1–5 (2011)
12. Nishikawa, N., et al.: High-performance symmetric block ciphers on multicore CPU and GPUs. Int. J. Networking Comput. **2**(2), 251–268 (2012)
13. Sanz, V. et al.: Comparison of Hardware and Software Implementations of AES on Shared-Memory Architectures. In: Proceedings of the 2021 Conference on Cloud Computing, Big Data & Emerging Topics. CCIS book Series, vol. 1444, pp. 60–70 (2021)
14. Fei, X., et al.: A secure and efficient file protecting system based on SHA3 and parallel AES. Parall. Comput. **52**, 106–132 (2016)
15. Top 500. https://www.top500.org/
16. Green 500. https://www.top500.org/lists/green500/
17. Guao, G., et al.: Different implementations of AES cryptographic algorithm. In: Proceedings of the 2015 IEEE 17th International Conference on High Performance Computing and Communications, pp. 1848–1853 (2015)
18. Kirk, D., et al.: Programming Massively Parallel Processors, 3rd edn. Morgan Kaufmann, Burlington, pp. 275–304 (2017)
19. Wan, L., et al.: Efficient CPU-GPU cooperative computing for solving the subset-sum problem. Concurrency Comput. Pract. Exp. **28**(2), 185–186 (2016)

Network Traffic Monitor for IDS in IoT

Diego Angelo Bolatti[ID], Carolina Todt[ID], Reinaldo Scappini[ID],
and Sergio Gramajo[✉][ID]

Resistencia Regional Faculty (UTN-FRRe), Center for Applied Research in Information and
Communication Technologies at National University of Technology (UTN), French Street 414,
Resistencia, Province of Chaco, Argentina
{dbolatti,carolinatodt,rscappini,
sergiogramajo}@gfe.frre.utn.edu.ar

Abstract. As network services and IoT technologies rapidly evolve, in literature there are many anomalies detection proposals based on datasets to deal with
cybersecurity threats. Most of this proposal uses structured data classification and
they can recognize with a certain degree of accuracy whether a type of traffic
is "anomalous" or not. Even what kind of anomaly it has. Nevertheless, previous
works do not clearly indicate the technical methodology to set up the data gathered
scenarios. As a main contribution, we are going to show a detailed deployment IoT
traffic monitor ready for intelligent network traffic classification. Monitoring and
sniffers are an essential concept in network management as it helps network operators to determine the network behavior and status of its components. Anomaly
detection also depends on monitoring for decision-making. Thus, this paper will
describe the creation of a portable network traffic monitor for IoT using Docker
container and bridge networking with SDN.

Keywords: Network monitoring · IoT · IDS · SDN

1 Introduction

Nowadays, as technology becomes more widely available, millions of users worldwide
have used some type of smart device. The number of smart homes in Europe and North
America has reached 102.6 million in 2020 and it will be 179 million in 2024 [1]. At
the same time more sophisticated IoT applications are deploying, and they use devices,
sensors, smart techniques to bring information or knowledge or, even, make decisions
[2, 3]. In a broad sense, this concept is Internet of Things (IoT) [4, 5] that was the result
of conventional network evolution connecting millions of devices with minimal human
intervention to later make any kind of decisions [6–8].

This has left the IoT vulnerable to various types of security threats just like other
technologies [9, 10]. In an effort to address these issues, different Intrusion Detection Systems (IDS) techniques have been proposed. Currently anomaly-based network
intrusion detection is an important field of research [11, 12].

In this way, Intrusion Detection Systems analyze network traffic to detect malicious
behavior. For its deployment it is necessary (i) Collect information; (ii) Analyze the

E. Rucci et al. (Eds.): JCC-BD&ET 2022, CCIS 1634, pp. 43–57, 2022.
https://doi.org/10.1007/978-3-031-14599-5_4

information; (iii) Identify threats or normal traffic through security events; and (iv) Detect and report threats [13]. The implementation described in this paper is focused only on point (i).

Many times, free open-source network sniffers are used to capture network traffic data and then, this data is labeled as a type of attack or normal traffic in an off-line way with datasets. Different types of intelligent approaches have been used like Machine Learning [14–16] and Deep Learning [17–22] in order to identify and classify threats. However, there is a lack of information about how an efficient IoT-based datasets scenario is obtained [23–29].

This work will not cover the complete development of an intelligent anomaly detection system for IoT, here we will show the theoretical fundaments and the basic elements to create a scenario to collect information from the IoT infrastructure, elaborated as the first part of the research project called "Intelligent Anomaly Detection System for IoT" [30] and part of the Technical Report "Proposal" presented at the International Telecommunications Union [31].

The remainder of the paper is structured as follows: Network Traffic Monitor Architecture is introduced in Sect. 2. A detailed description of deployment proposed is given in Sect. 3. Section 4 introduces the creation of an SDN Controller and traffic gathering. The conclusions and future work are given in Sect. 5.

2   Network Traffic Monitor Architecture

In principle, it is necessary to define the scope in which the proof of concept is created. Figure 1 shows the proposed architecture in four layers: device layer with Software Defined Network (SND) switch [32] and gateway with Openflow monitor where our proposal is deployment.

To design the monitoring system, we base our work on the following 3 concepts:

Namespace: a namespace in computer science is an abstract container or environment created to hold a logical grouping of unique identifiers or symbols (i.e. names).

Docker: is an open-source project that automates the deployment of applications inside software containers, by providing an additional layer of abstraction and automation of operating-system-level virtualization on Linux [33]. Docker uses the resource isolation features of the Linux kernel such as *cgroups* and kernel namespaces, and a union-capable file system such as aufs and others to allow independent "containers" to run within a single Linux instance, avoiding the overhead of starting and maintaining virtual machines. The Linux kernel's support for namespaces mostly isolates an application's view of the operating environment, including process trees, network, user IDs and mounted file systems, while the kernel's *cgroups* provide resource limiting, including the CPU, memory, block I/O and network. Since version 0.9, Docker includes the *libcontainer* library as its own way to directly use virtualization facilities provided by the Linux kernel, in addition to using abstracted virtualization interfaces via *libvirt*, LXC (Linux Containers) and *systemd-nspawn*. Docker perfectly adjusts the needs of our work, because it can be implemented in the same way, both in a testing and simulation environment within a virtual machine, or in a production environment, on local servers, cloud servers, etc.

Connectivity Network with Docker: when installing Docker on an operating system, it creates a bridge to a network called *docker0*, and this network connects by default all containers, unless otherwise indicated. If a virtual machine with Docker is used, it is necessary to configure the network understanding that it is necessary to work with different levels of abstraction. In the case of containers (they have their own namespace), it will be necessary to connect them to the virtual machine where they are running, and this, in turn, to the host, to the Internet, and/or to other virtual machines if they exist. Figure 2 shows in the shaded box, the concrete boundaries of the implementation of the access module to the proposed IoT architecture. It is then understood that it is implemented in the operating system that supports the IoT Gateway and the traffic switching and monitoring module.

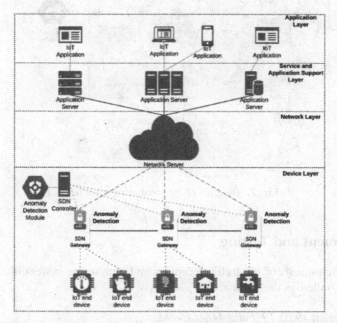

Fig. 1. Architecture of the intelligent anomaly detection system for IoT.

The implementation of the switching and traffic monitoring module is described in detail below, highlighting that the implementation makes no difference, whether it is carried out in a virtual machine environment or in a production environment directly on the host operating system (usually Linux). This is due to the characteristic of isolation that namespaces have, which allows a great portability. Another issue in this design is that the SDN controller and the Machine Learning module have absolute independence in terms of their physical location; it is enough to properly define the corresponding communication channel. Basically, the scenario in which we worked to realize the design and testing of the proposed architecture is a computer that we call a base machine, with an O.S. Ubuntu 20.04 and a virtualization system VirtualBox Version 6.1.10_Ubuntu r138449. In addition, we use a Virtual Machine (VM) named "*iot*" configured with Ubuntu 20.04 OS.

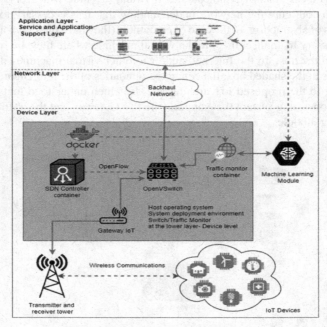

Fig. 2. Diagram of the monitoring system.

3 Deployment and Testing

To test the components of the traffic reception and monitoring system, the following software is installed on the VM iot:

- Docker *version 19.03.13, build 4484c46d9d.*
- Open *vSwitch version 2.13.0.*

With this software, you can use containers and manage traffic with an OpenFlow switch (OpenvSwitch). The outline of the study scenario is shown in Fig. 3 (a).

The components of the study topology comprise an SDN controller, an OpenFlow switch that performs the functions of managing traffic, two hosts called Host1 and Host2, which are intended for different connectivity tests, and a container called Monitor, which includes the appropriate software to capture traffic. The base machine has a physical Ethernet interface called *enp0s2* and a network of the VirtualBox hypervisor, *vboxnet0* and *vboxnet1* respectively (Fig. 3. (b)).

Four networks are defined, three of which are managed by the VirtualBox hypervisor and one by Docker. A bridge type network with *enp0s3* interface linked to the *enp0s2* interface of the base machine, this allows sending and receiving traffic to and from all the

VM devices. A connection to the *vboxnet0 192.168.56.0/24* network with a host-only interface (called *enp0s8* on the VM). A *vboxnet1 192.168.1.0/24* network connection with a host-only interface (called enp0s9 in the VM). Docker manages by default a network that allows it to connect the containers by assigning ip addresses using *dhcp* on the *172.17.0.0/24* network. Initially, we check the status of the interfaces in the VM iot.

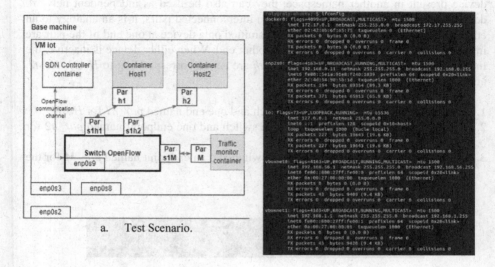

a.   Test Scenario.

b.   Initial configuration of VM iot.

Fig. 3. Deployment scenario.

Linux supports individual network namespaces, each host has a default *netns*, named by default, and each host container is isolated into its *netns* that are identified by an integer.

In the next subsections we will review in detail the important preliminary aspects before creating the monitor.

3.1 Creating Topology Elements. OpenFlow Switch

The next step is to configure the *ovs* Linux switch by executing the following commands:

sudo ovs-vsctl add-br s1
sudo ifconfig enp0s9 0
sudo ovs-vsctl add-port s1 enp0s9
sudo ifconfig s1 192.168.1.11/24

With these commands an OpenFlow switch called *s1* was created. To which the interface *enp0s9* was added and *s1* was configured with the ip *192.168.1.11/24*.

3.2   Creating Links Between Components

To make the corresponding connections between the different components of our scenario we will make use of a feature provided by the Linux kernel called virtual Ethernet link (*veth*), these virtual Ethernet devices can act as tunnels between network namespaces, or they are used to create a bridge to a physical environment with a network device present in another namespace, they can also be used as independent network devices. *Veth* devices are always created in interconnected pairs, it is an analogy to an ethernet cable with two ends. Packets transmitted on a device at one end of the pair are immediately received at the device at the other end. When either device is inactive, the link state of the peer is inactive. Three *veth* are added corresponding to *Host1, Host2*, and *Monitor* respectively (see Fig. 4):

1. One end named *par_s1h1* for the switch and one end named *par_h1* for *Host1*.
2. One endpoint named *par_s1h2* for the switch and one endpoint named *par_h2* for *Host2*.
3. An endpoint named *par_s1M* for the switch and an endpoint named *par_M* for the Monitor.

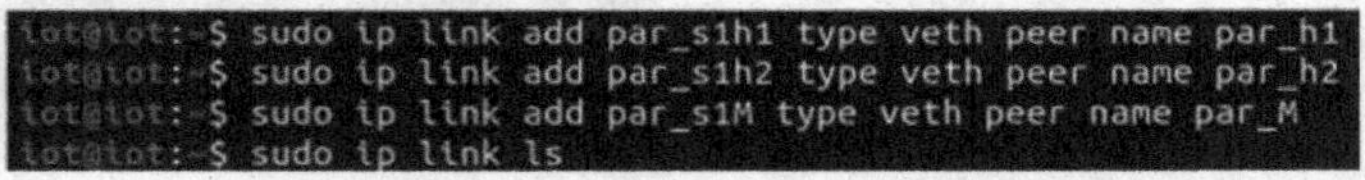

```
iot@iot:~$ sudo ip link add par_s1h1 type veth peer name par_h1
iot@iot:~$ sudo ip link add par_s1h2 type veth peer name par_h2
iot@iot:~$ sudo ip link add par_s1M type veth peer name par_M
iot@iot:~$ sudo ip link ls
```

Fig. 4.   Ethernet links of the global space.

The endpoints of the corresponding virtual links created are incorporated into switch s1 as ports and the interfaces are up (Fig. 5 (a)).

Next, we will create the other elements we need within the topology, using Docker. Then, from the local Docker repository images in the VM, we start a container named 1.0 to monitor the traffic. To obtain the configuration of the monitor interfaces, run the following command (Fig. 5 (b)).

3.3   Connecting the Monitor

We open another terminal in the VM and obtain the PID of the container, with the *inspect* command of Docker, which returns low-level information of the Docker objects. In order to do this, the list of processes in Docker is queried with the docker *ps* command (Fig. 5 (c)).

Then ***docker inspect -f '{{.State.Pid}}' 14cb73456d20***. returns as the result: *2051*.

To move the par_M endpoint into the monitor namespace *run:**sudo ip link set par_M netns 2051***. Then we execute the following command: ***sudo ln -s /proc/2051/ns/net /var/run/netns/2051***. Then directly from the VM terminal we can comfortably do ip netns exec (namespace) (command to execute in the namespace). In our case: ***sudo ip netns exec 2051 ip link list*** (Fig. 6).

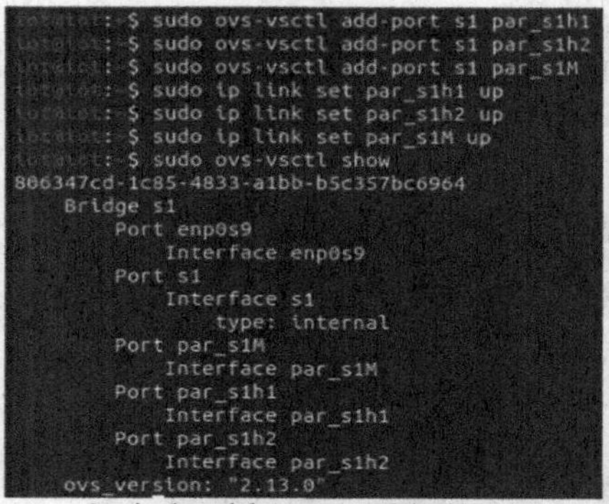

a. Switch with ports added.

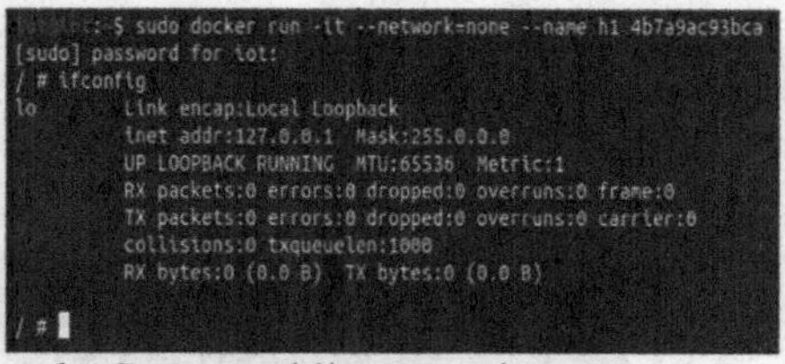

b. Command line container *Cont1*.

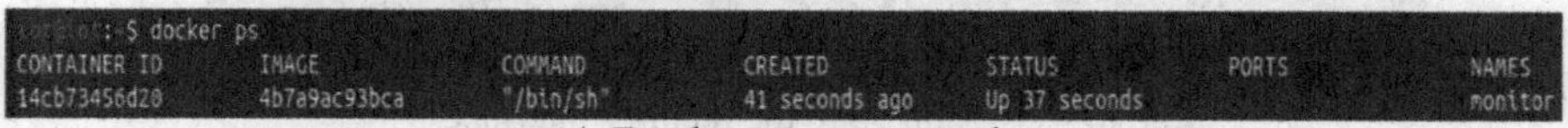

c. Docker *ps* command.

Fig. 5. Commands.

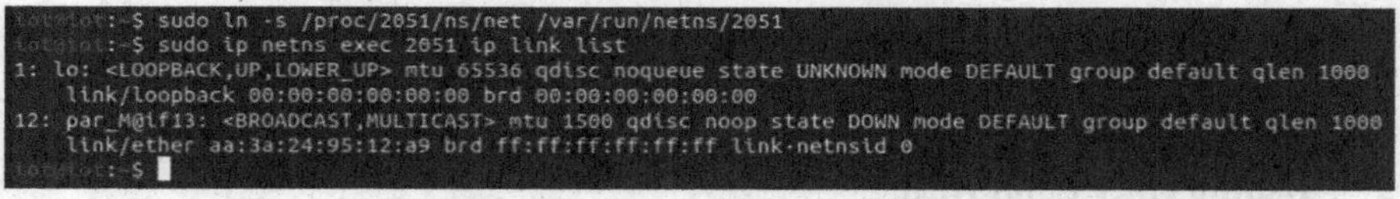

Fig. 6. Virtual link to the directory containing the namespace monitor.

We continue the scenario assembly by assigning in the monitor container the name eth1 to the end par_M. Then we assign as interface name eth1 the par_M name on the monitor as follows: *sudo ip netns exec 2051 ip link set dev par_M name eth1*, the interface is activated: *sudo ip netns exec 2051 ip link set eth1 up*. In the monitor namespace you can check the result of these last two actions as shown in Fig. 7.

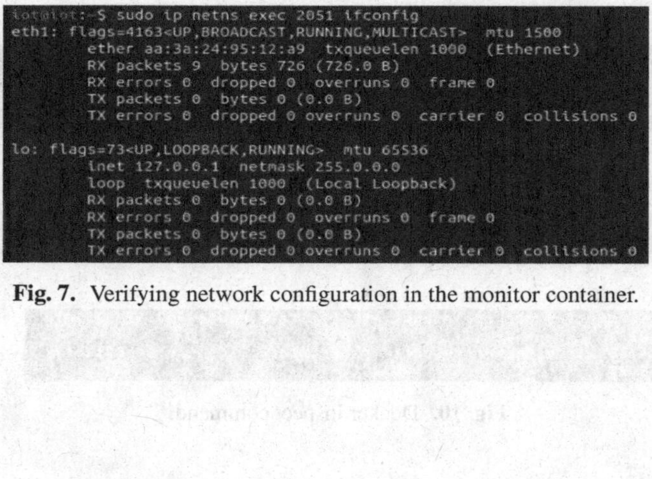

Fig. 7. Verifying network configuration in the monitor container.

In the monitor assign to eth1 an ip address of the network connected to the ovs switch (which in our case is the vboxnet1 192.168.1.0/24 network): *sudo ip netns exec 2051 ifconfig eth1 192.168.1.221/24* then verify again in the monitor (Fig. 8).

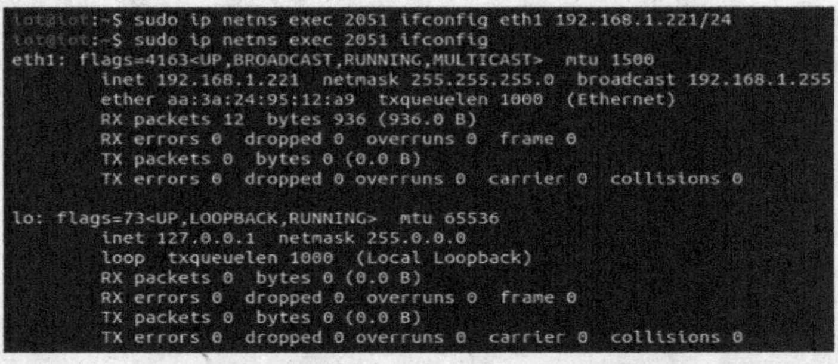

```
iot@iot:~$ sudo ip netns exec 2051 ifconfig eth1 192.168.1.221/24
iot@iot:~$ sudo ip netns exec 2051 ifconfig
eth1: flags=4163<UP,BROADCAST,RUNNING,MULTICAST>  mtu 1500
        inet 192.168.1.221  netmask 255.255.255.0  broadcast 192.168.1.255
        ether aa:3a:24:95:12:a9  txqueuelen 1000  (Ethernet)
        RX packets 12  bytes 936 (936.0 B)
        RX errors 0  dropped 0  overruns 0  frame 0
        TX packets 0  bytes 0 (0.0 B)
        TX errors 0  dropped 0 overruns 0  carrier 0  collisions 0

lo: flags=73<UP,LOOPBACK,RUNNING>  mtu 65536
        inet 127.0.0.1  netmask 255.0.0.0
        loop  txqueuelen 1000  (Local Loopback)
        RX packets 0  bytes 0 (0.0 B)
        RX errors 0  dropped 0  overruns 0  frame 0
        TX packets 0  bytes 0 (0.0 B)
        TX errors 0  dropped 0 overruns 0  carrier 0  collisions 0
```

Fig. 8. Assigning ip to the monitor interface.

As you can see the monitor now has an ethernet interface with the name *eth1*, the ip *192.168.1.221/24* and is connected to the switch port named *par_s1M*. At this point, we have added an OpenFlow switch named *s1* and a container named monitor into the scenario and connected them together.

3.4   Creating Host 1 and Host 2

First we create the containers Host1 and Host2, based on the Linux Alpine image we have available in the local repository with the *ID:a24bb4013296: docker run -itd --name = cont1 --net = none a24bb4013296*.

3.5   Connecting Host 1 and Host 2

As can be seen in the Fig. 9, the containers were created and were running in the background.

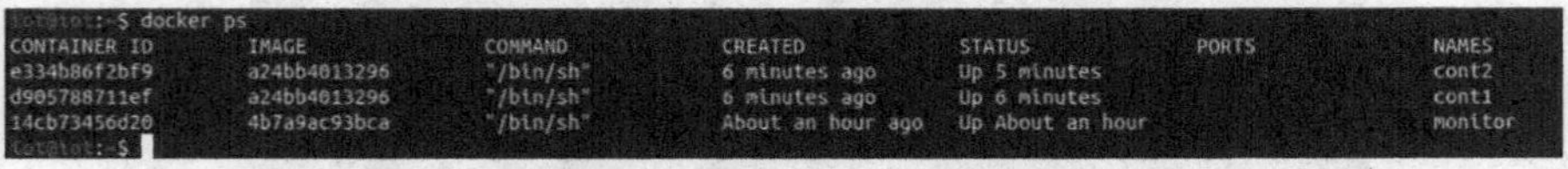

```
iot@iot:~$ docker ps
CONTAINER ID   IMAGE          COMMAND      CREATED          STATUS           PORTS    NAMES
e334b86f2bf9   a24bb4013296   "/bin/sh"    6 minutes ago    Up 5 minutes              cont2
d905788711ef   a24bb4013296   "/bin/sh"    6 minutes ago    Up 6 minutes              cont1
14cb73456d20   4b7a9ac93bca   "/bin/sh"    About an hour ago Up About an hour         monitor
iot@iot:~$
```

Fig. 9. Processes running in docker.

At this point we can find out the respective namespaces (Fig. 10).

```
iot@iot:~$ docker inspect -f '{{.State.Pid}}' d905788711ef
2371
iot@iot:~$ docker inspect -f '{{.State.Pid}}' e334b86f2bf9
2420
```

Fig. 10. Docker inspect command.

As shown in Fig. 10, the Host1 namespace is *2371*, and the *Host2* namespace is *2420*.

- To move the par_h1 endpoint into the Host1 namespace, you run: ***sudo ip link set par_h1 netns 2371***.
- To move the par_h2 endpoint into the Host2 namespace run: ***sudo ip link set par_h1 netns 2420***.

Next, virtual links are created to the /proc directory:

sudo ln -s /proc/2371/ns/net /var/run/netns/2371

sudo ln -s /proc/2420/ns/net /var/run/netns/2420

We proceed to verify that the endpoints are in the respective spaces (Fig. 11).

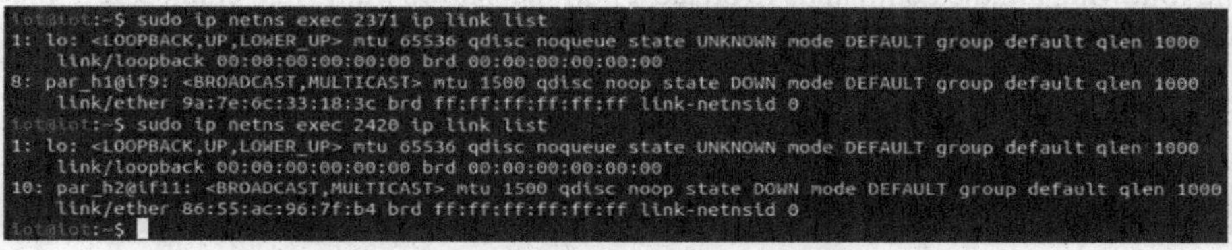

```
iot@iot:~$ sudo ip netns exec 2371 ip link list
1: lo: <LOOPBACK,UP,LOWER_UP> mtu 65536 qdisc noqueue state UNKNOWN mode DEFAULT group default qlen 1000
    link/loopback 00:00:00:00:00:00 brd 00:00:00:00:00:00
8: par_h1@if9: <BROADCAST,MULTICAST> mtu 1500 qdisc noop state DOWN mode DEFAULT group default qlen 1000
    link/ether 9a:7e:6c:33:18:3c brd ff:ff:ff:ff:ff:ff link-netnsid 0
iot@iot:~$ sudo ip netns exec 2420 ip link list
1: lo: <LOOPBACK,UP,LOWER_UP> mtu 65536 qdisc noqueue state UNKNOWN mode DEFAULT group default qlen 1000
    link/loopback 00:00:00:00:00:00 brd 00:00:00:00:00:00
10: par_h2@if11: <BROADCAST,MULTICAST> mtu 1500 qdisc noop state DOWN mode DEFAULT group default qlen 1000
    link/ether 86:55:ac:96:7f:b4 brd ff:ff:ff:ff:ff:ff link-netnsid 0
iot@iot:~$
```

Fig. 11. Verification of links on Host1 and Host2 netns.

As shown in the figure, par_h1 is in the *Host1* space, and *par_h2* in the *Host2* space. Then we proceed to give them name and interface (*eth1*) corresponding ip address and raise them to be active and set the corresponding ip. The complete sequence is shown in Fig. 12.

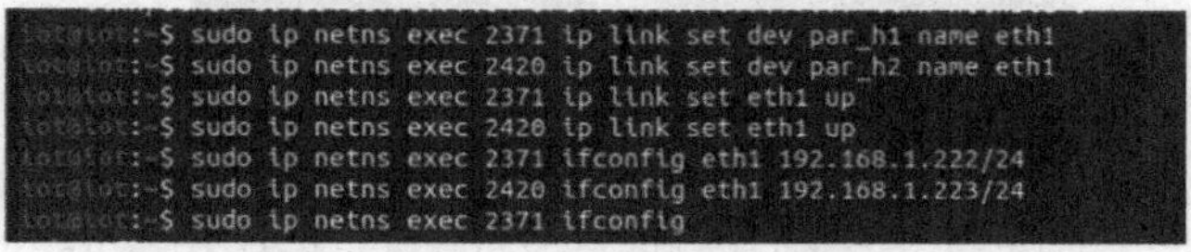

```
iot@iot:~$ sudo ip netns exec 2371 ip link set dev par_h1 name eth1
iot@iot:~$ sudo ip netns exec 2420 ip link set dev par_h2 name eth1
iot@iot:~$ sudo ip netns exec 2371 ip link set eth1 up
iot@iot:~$ sudo ip netns exec 2420 ip link set eth1 up
iot@iot:~$ sudo ip netns exec 2371 ifconfig eth1 192.168.1.222/24
iot@iot:~$ sudo ip netns exec 2420 ifconfig eth1 192.168.1.223/24
iot@iot:~$ sudo ip netns exec 2371 ifconfig
```

Fig. 12. Host1 and Host2 network configuration.

4   Creating SDN Controller and Traffic Sniffer

Now it is time to add the SDN controller to the topology and connect it to the switch to manage it, for this we have in the local docker repository an image with a version of the onos SDN controller, with *ID: c07e43df3bf2*.

We execute the following command to run the SDN controller and access to its interface: ***docker run -itd -p 6653:6653 -p 8181:8181 -p 8101:8101 -p 5005:5005 -p 830:830 --name = onos c07e43df3bf2***.

Once logged in onos, two applications are added: Open Flow Provider Suite and Reactive Forwarding. Once the controller is running, the switch is connected to it in order to be able to install flow rules through it. Tell the switch s1 which version of OpenFlow it is going to operate with: *sudo ovs-vsctl set bridge s1 protocols = Open-Flow13* and connect switch s1 to the controller using: *sudo ovs-vsctl set-controller s1 tcp:192.168.56.11:6653*.

Keep in mind that 192.168.56.0 is the vboxnet0 network and thanks to have configured a bridge network in VirtualBox, we can have communication with all networks that we have configured in the MV iot, thanks to this also works port forwarding docker and we can use the browser of the base machine to access them. Once this point is reached, you can operate the switch at low level via terminal with the commands provided by *ovs-vsctl* and *ovs-ofctl*.

Traffic Capture Function. OVS provides a way to duplicate network traffic from specific ports to a dedicated outgoing port. The duplication can be in one direction or both. The following are the commands to create a port that shows traffic and connect it to the monitor container for processing purposes. First, create the mirror port on the switch (Fig. 13).

```
iotiot:-$ sudo ovs-vsctl -- --id=@m create mirror name=espejo -- add bridge s1 mirrors @m
[sudo] password for iot:
71940157-4e43-4bc3-846a-2440d851fa06
```

Fig. 13. Inserting mirror port on the switch.

Next, we will get the uuids of the ports we are interested in for the switch configuration by mirroring the desired traffic to the monitor port (Fig. 14).

```
iotiot:-$ sudo ovs-vsctl get port "enp0s9" _uuid
5cbd9cd2-8164-42dd-95b9-5bb07085c2a0
iotiot:-$ sudo ovs-vsctl get port "par_s1h1" _uuid
9fdd1399-2d78-455a-a50a-bb61b3e994db
iotiot:-$ sudo ovs-vsctl get port "par_s1h2" _uuid
5b8ee856-1b28-4e4d-8dcf-122bcced7d6f
iotiot:-$ sudo ovs-vsctl get port "par_s1M" _uuid
b9e505e4-5694-4f0c-b4f7-39209a5122e1
iotiot:-$ 
```

Fig. 14. Obtaining the uuid of the switch s1 ports.

With this information we can configure which are the ports whose inbound and/or outbound traffic we want to show. To do this we execute the following command:

sudo ovs-vsctl set mirror espejo select_src_port = 9fdd1399-2d78-455a-a50a-bb61b3e994db,5b8ee856-1b28-4e4d-8dcf-122bcced7d6f select_dst_port = 9fdd1399-2d78-455a-a50a-bb61b3e994db,5b8ee856-1b28-4e4d-8dcf-122bcced7d6f

With the above command we inform the switch that we want all traffic exchange in both directions from the ports that are connected to Host1 and Host2. We verify the configuration as follows: *sudo ovs-vsctl list mirror mirror*.

Now all that remains is to inform which port will be the outgoing port for the duplicated traffic using the command: *ovs-vsctl -- --id =* @(uuid corresponding to the output) get port (uuid corresponding to the output) *-- set mirror mirror output-port =* @(uuid corresponding to the output).

sudo ovs-vsctl -- --id = @b9e505e4–5694-4f0c-b4f7-39209a5122e1 get port b9e505e4– 5694-4f0c-b4f7-39209a5122e1 -- set mirror mirror output-port = @b9e505e4–5694- 4f0c-b4f7-39209a5122e1

There you can see the outgoing port for the duplicated traffic, which is the port that corresponds to the connection with the monitor. Under these conditions, we can test generating traffic between Host1 and Host2, and see if we can capture it in the monitor container, for that we run in a terminal the command ***docker* ps** to identify the process where the monitor is running and then with the command ***docker exec -it (process)* sh**, returns us a terminal with command line inside the monitor container and once there we configure a data capture with tcpdump (Fig. 15).

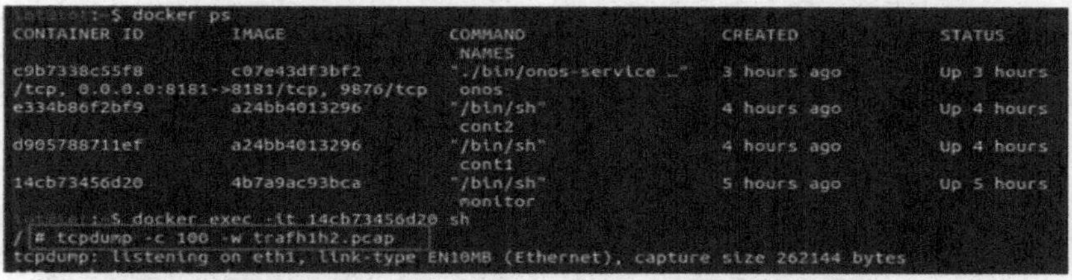

Fig. 15. Configuration of traffic capture inside the monitor container.

As you can see, a capture of 100 frames was configured and saved in a file named trafh1h2.pcap. We also do the same by opening a terminal on h1 and pinging h2 to generate a sample traffic (Fig. 16).

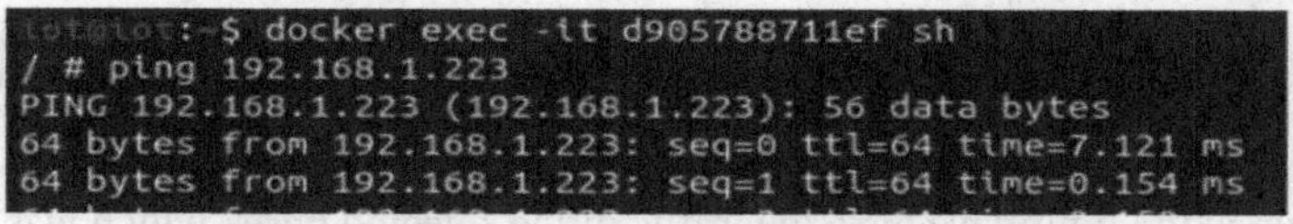

Fig. 16. Generating traffic from Host1 to Host2.

This generates continuous traffic between *cont1* and *cont2*, and in the monitor container a file is generated containing the capture of the traffic between *cont1* and *cont2*, reflected in the port of connection of the monitor to the OpenFlow switch as shown in Fig. 17.

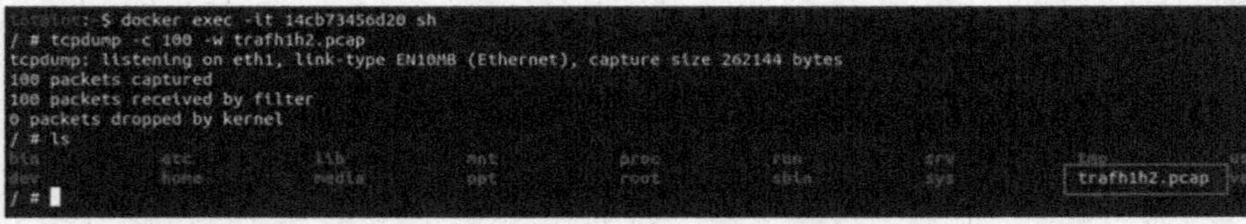

Fig. 17. Capture file generated on the monitor.

Once the capture file is generated we copy it from the container to the MV iot with the command: ***docker cp monitor:/trafh1h2.pcap***. Then from the MV iot to the base machine in the Documents folder to be able to analyze it with Wireshark with: ***scp iot@192.168.56.11:/home/iot/trafh1h2.pcap Documents/***. And finally, we open the file with the capture to examine it (Fig. 18).

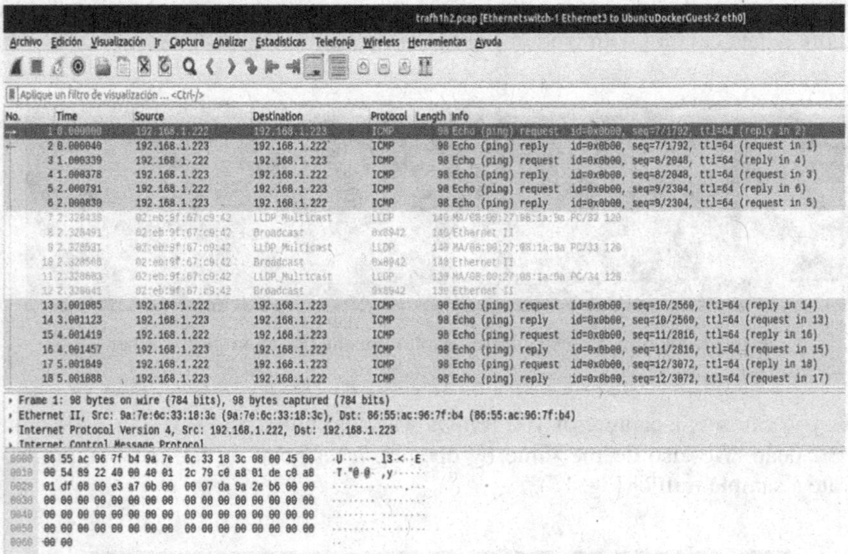

Fig. 18. Wireshark screen displaying the file with the data capture performed.

As shown in the figure, we have the traffic of the selected ports, which was captured by the monitor container. In the same way, we can proceed to select any interface and type of traffic because the design is flexible to adapt to any scenario and has the advantage of being "portable". The example traffic between two generic hosts was chosen, to represent the input and output of backbone traffic, as it could perfectly be representing the output of the IoT Gateway in its transit to the network backhaul. This work describes all the low-level engineering to build the scenario, analyzing all the functional components and connectivity.

5   Conclusions and Future Work

In this work, we show the design and implementation of an IoT network monitoring system that provides network traffic data and statistics for the top layer of the IoT architecture. The results of the experiment show the feasibility of the traffic monitoring system and its application in the device layer of the IoT architecture. As a tutorial, it has been shown step by step how to create an architecture for data capture with an IoT platform based on traffic analyzers and SDN from a scenario divided into abstraction layers. This work is the baseline for the collection of robust data that will later become part of IDS and learning methods for network traffic classification.

It is essential to mention that this work deals with the study and implementation of the capture module, from the lowest level acting directly on the linux kernel, it aims to show in a didactic way, acquire the "know how" to understand higher level developments and with greater ease of implementation, offering a fully modular and scalable solution with the possibility of using orchestration tools, such as Kubernetes, Terraform, etc. We want to highlight the introductory nature of this document based on this objective.

In accordance with the above, with a view to continuing this work, and with the aim of improving the performance of the traffic monitor shown here, we will soon publish the progress we made in the design of a monitoring module which a concept of "promiscuous bridge", designed from a bridge and a Docker container that contains the capture software tcpdump with all the advantages of capturing in "raw" mode, capturing all the packets of a given interface reflected in the bridge interface at which the monitor is connected. By capturing all the traffic of the chosen interface, the bridge also allows multiple tools to obtain the same data, which is very useful; if, for example, you want to define traffic selection and filter functions, a fundamental requirement for the development of an IDS. It should be noted that the use of Docker provides an isolated and easily replicable environment that ensures portability and implementation of the monitor wherever it is needed.

References

1. Berg Insight: IoT Business News, https://iotbusinessnews.com/2021/02/11/06951-the-num ber-of-smart-homes-in-europe-and-north-america-will-reach-179-million-in-2024/
2. Zhang, J., Tao, D.: Empowering things with intelligence: a survey of the progress, challenges, and opportunities in artificial intelligence of things. IEEE Internet Things J. **8**, 7789–7817 (2021). https://doi.org/10.1109/JIOT.2020.3039359
3. Barreto, L., Amaral, A., Pereira, T.: Industry 4.0 implications in logistics: an overview. Procedia Manuf. **13**, 1245–1252 (2017). https://doi.org/10.1016/j.promfg.2017.09.045
4. Ashton, K.: That 'internet of things' thing. RFID J. **22**(7), 97–114 (2009)
5. Madakam, S., Lake, V., Lake, V., Lake, V.: Internet of things (IoT): a literature review. J. Comput. Commun. **3**(05), 164 (2015). https://doi.org/10.4236/jcc.2015.35021
6. Silva, B.N., Khan, M., Han, K.: Internet of things: a comprehensive review of enabling technologies, architecture, and challenges. IETE Tech. Rev. **35**, 205–220 (2018). https://doi. org/10.1080/02564602.2016.1276416
7. Gubbi, J., Buyya, R., Marusic, S., Palaniswami, M.: Internet of Things (IoT): a vision, archi- tectural elements, and future directions. Future Gener. Comput. Syst. **29**, 1645–1660 (2013). https://doi.org/10.1016/j.future.2013.01.010

8. Louis, J., Dunston, P.S.: Integrating IoT into operational workflows for real-time and auto-mated decision-making in repetitive construction operations. Autom. Constr. **94**, 317–327 (2018). https://doi.org/10.1016/j.autcon.2018.07.005

9. Al-Hadhrami, Y., Hussain, F.K.: Real time dataset generation framework for intrusion detection systems in IoT. Future Gener. Comput. Syst. **108**, 414–423 (2020). https://doi.org/10.1016/j.future.2020.02.051

10. Borgohain, T., Kumar, U., Sanyal, S.: Survey of security and privacy issues of internet of things. ArXiv150102211 Cs. (2015)

11. Ferrag, M.A., Maglaras, L., Moschoyiannis, S., Janicke, H.: Deep learning for cyber security intrusion detection: Approaches, datasets, and comparative study. J. Inf. Secur. Appl. **50**, 102419 (2020). https://doi.org/10.1016/j.jisa.2019.102419

12. Eskandari, M., Janjua, Z.H., Vecchio, M., Antonelli, F.: Passban IDS: an intelligent anomaly-based intrusion detection system for IoT edge devices. IEEE Internet Things J. **7**, 6882–6897 (2020). https://doi.org/10.1109/JIOT.2020.2970501

13. Chaabouni, N., Mosbah, M., Zemmari, A., Sauvignac, C., Faruki, P.: Network intrusion detection for IoT security based on learning techniques. IEEE Commun. Surv. Tutor. **21**, 2671–2701 (2019). https://doi.org/10.1109/COMST.2019.2896380

14. Özgür, A., Erdem, H.: A review of KDD99 dataset usage in intrusion detection and machine learning between 2010 and 2015. PeerJ Inc. (2016). https://doi.org/10.7287/peerj.preprints.1954v1

15. Jan, S.U., Ahmed, S., Shakhov, V., Koo, I.: Toward a lightweight intrusion detection system for the internet of things. IEEE Access. **7**, 42450–42471 (2019). https://doi.org/10.1109/ACCESS.2019.2907965

16. Hsu, C.-W., Chang, C.-C., Lin, C.-J.: A practical guide to support vector classification **16** (2003)

17. Xu, C., Shen, J., Du, X., Zhang, F.: An Intrusion detection system using a deep neural network with gated recurrent units. IEEE Access. **6**, 48697–48707 (2018). https://doi.org/10.1109/ACCESS.2018.2867564

18. Yin, C., Zhu, Y., Fei, J., He, X.: A Deep learning approach for intrusion detection using recurrent neural networks. IEEE Access. **5**, 21954–21961 (2017). https://doi.org/10.1109/ACCESS.2017.2762418

19. Li, Z., Qin, Z., Huang, K., Yang, X., Ye, S.: Intrusion detection using convolutional neural networks for representation learning. In: Liu, D., Xie, S., Li, Y., Zhao, D., El-Alfy, E.-S. (eds.) ICONIP 2017. LNCS, vol. 10638, pp. 858–866. Springer, Cham (2017). https://doi.org/10.1007/978-3-319-70139-4_87

20. Vinayakumar, R., Soman, K.P., Poornachandran, P.: Applying convolutional neural network for network intrusion detection. In: 2017 International Conference on Advances in Computing, Communications and Informatics (ICACCI), pp. 1222–1228 (2017). https://doi.org/10.1109/ICACCI.2017.8126009

21. Collective anomaly detection based on long short-term memory recurrent neural networks. https://doi.org/10.1007/978-3-319-48057-2_9. Accessed 15 Mar 2022

22. Roy, S.S., Mallik, A., Gulati, R., Obaidat, M.S., Krishna, P.V.: A deep learning based artificial neural network approach for intrusion detection. In: Giri, D., Mohapatra, R.N., Begehr, H., Obaidat, M.S. (eds.) ICMC 2017. CCIS, vol. 655, pp. 44–53. Springer, Singapore (2017). https://doi.org/10.1007/978-981-10-4642-1_5

23. Koroniotis, N., Moustafa, N., Sitnikova, E., Turnbull, B.: Towards the development of realistic botnet dataset in the Internet of things for network forensic analytics: bot-IoT dataset. Future Gener. Comput. Syst. **100**, 779–796 (2019). https://doi.org/10.1016/j.future.2019.05.041

24. Ashraf, J., et al.: IoTBoT-IDS: a novel statistical learning-enabled botnet detection framework for protecting networks of smart cities. Sustain. Cities Soc. **72**, 103041 (2021). https://doi.org/10.1016/j.scs.2021.103041

25. Alsaedi, A., Moustafa, N., Tari, Z., Mahmood, A., Anwar, A.: TON_IoT telemetry dataset: a new generation dataset of IoT and IIoT for data-driven intrusion detection systems. IEEE Access **8**, 165130–165150 (2020). https://doi.org/10.1109/ACCESS.2020.3022862
26. Moustafa, N., Ahmed, M., Ahmed, S.: Data Analytics-enabled intrusion detection: evaluations of ToN_IoT Linux datasets. In: 2020 IEEE 19th International Conference on Trust, Security and Privacy in Computing and Communications (TrustCom), pp. 727–735 (2020). https://doi.org/10.1109/TrustCom50675.2020.00100
27. Garcia, S., Parmisano, A., Erquiaga, M.J.: IoT-23: a labeled dataset with malicious and benign IoT network traffic (2020). https://zenodo.org/record/4743746. https://doi.org/10.5281/zenodo.4743746
28. Abdalgawad, N., Sajun, A., Kaddoura, Y., Zualkernan, I.A., Aloul, F.: Generative deep learning to detect cyberattacks for the IoT-23 dataset. IEEE Access. **10**, 6430–6441 (2022). https://doi.org/10.1109/ACCESS.2021.3140015
29. K., Geetha, K., Brahmananda, S.H.: Network traffic analysis through deep learning for detection of an army of bots in health IoT network. Int. J. Pervasive Comput. Commun. (2022). https://doi.org/10.1108/IJPCC-10-2021-0259
30. Bolatti, D., Karanik, M., Todt, C., Scappini, R., Gramajo, S.: Intelligent anomaly detection system for IoT. In: IX Jornadas de Cloud Computing, Big Data & Emerging Topics, pp. 47–50. Universidad Nacional de La Plata, La Plata (2021)
31. Bolatti, D., Todt, C., Karanik, M., Scappini, R.: Proposed update of technical report ITU-T YSTR-IADIoT. Intell. Anomaly Detect. Syst. IoT, https://www.itu.int/md/T17-SG020RG.LATAM-C-0014/en. Accessed 14 Apr 2022
32. Elsayed, M.S., Le-Khac, N.-A., Jurcut, A.D.: InSDN: a novel SDN intrusion dataset. IEEE Access. **8**, 165263–165284 (2020). https://doi.org/10.1109/ACCESS.2020.3022633
33. Docker Documentation. https://docs.docker.com/. Accessed 14 Apr 2022

Crane: A Local Deployment Tool
for Containerized Applications

Jose Arcidiacono[1]([⊠]) [iD], Patricia Bazán[1] [iD], Nicolás del Río[1] [iD],
and Alejandra B. Lliteras[2,3] [iD]

[1] Facultad de Informática, LINTI, Universidad Nacional de La Plata, Calle 50 esquina 120S/N,
2° piso, La Plata, Argentina
jarcidiacono@linti.unlp.edu.ar, {pbaz,ndelrio}@info.unlp.edu.ar
[2] Facultad de Informática, LIFIA, Universidad Nacional de La Plata, Calle 50 esquina 120S/N,
1° piso, La Plata, Argentina
alejandra.lliteras@lifia.info.unlp.edu.ar
[3] CICPBA, Calle 526 e/10 y 11, La Plata, Argentina

Abstract. Application deployment as one of the software development stages has
become more complex in the presence of distributed architectures that involve a
variety of tools, and, with them, configuration differences, versioning and communication protocols. Even when cloud services have contributed a solution in
this sense, it is still difficult to deploy distributed applications in on-premise
environments.

The container concept as packages that include the application code, its dependencies, libraries and services required for its correct execution, turns out to be
an alternative for streamlining application deployment and it allows taking the
virtualization concept to the operative system. However, it adds a software layer
that requires monitoring and management.

There are robust solutions for administering and monitoring containers but
they also require computing resources that sometimes exceed the capacity of the
average computer used for development, and they make local deployment difficult.

In this work, the design of Crane, a tool for local deployment of containerized
applications is presented. This tool has the characteristic of being lightweight,
of general purpose and with automatic scaling capacities, which differentiates it
from the Minikube tool, which allows some local Kubernetes API testing and is
used mainly for the development of new features for the latter.

Keywords: Middleware framework · Container deployment · Distributed
services

1 Introduction

The responsibility to deploy and monitor applications traditionally fell on an administrator that knew about infrastructure and networking, and was dedicated specifically to this
task. With the advent of cloud services (PaaS, Platform as a Service) [1] monitoring and
metrics became available to developers. In addition, with the advancement of continuous

integration (CI) [2] and continuous delivery (CD) [3], a trend that proposes to test and deploy code as it is written, the deployment became closer to developers [4].

One aspect to be considered when deploying is the difference that exists between the developing, testing and production environments. This can lead to version problems –tool or library related–, configuration differences –e.g. connection timeouts–, and others.

One way to unify the environments is to use Docker[1], a container virtualization platform that allows creating "images" that include dependencies and configuration for an application. From a Docker image identical containers can be created, always with the same dependencies and initial configuration. Additionally, these containers can be parametrized. This means that each container can receive configurations as URLs to connect to, ports to open, and others. This configuration is in container creation time and it allows adapting (in a static way) the environment using console arguments or a simple text file. There are cloud platforms that support container use in production environments, both as unitary applications and as interconnected services.

When adding multiple containers the need to monitor and orchestrate them, that is, to define their start order and the dependencies between them, appears. One option to carry out these tasks automatically is Kubernetes[2], a container orchestration, monitoring and scaling platform. Kubernetes has the disadvantage of needing at least three virtual machines in order to work, and more machines can be added in order to increase the cluster count [5].

These specifications exceed the resources available in an average development machine, and because of that, are not suited for local deployment. There is a lightweight version, Minikube[3], that allows some local testing of the Kubernetes API and it is used mainly for development of new features for the main project.

In this context we present the design of Crane, a local deployment tool for Docker-containerized applications that, unlike Minikube, is a general-purpose tool and it has an automatic scaling feature. The presented work is organized as follows: 1– In Section "Container management architecture precedents" some container management solutions with scaling are describer. 2– In Section "Design evolution of Crane", our container management tool, Crane, is presented. 3– Section "Conclusions and future work" closes this work and extension points are enumerated.

2 Container Management Architecture Precedents

Even when container management and scaling is a new area and one in constant evolution, the investigation leading to this work reported an existing vacancy in terms of using this technology in one computer, through a management tool with capacity to scale for the administrator.

The state of art studied in this matter was exhaustive and went through several topics, but in order to address the Crane proposal, several solutions that allow container management and their scaling were surveyed and two of them were chosen for description and analysis: 1- SWITCH system [6] and 2- COCOS architecture [7], which is a

---

[1] https://www.docker.com/.

[2] https://kubernetes.io/.

[3] https://minikube.sigs.k8s.io/docs/.

Kubernetes extension. This selection is due both of them being complete architecture definitions addressing the problem.

2.1 SWITCH

SWITCH is an automatic scaling system for container based adaptable applications. In the article [6] presenting it, different metric types are studied for both vertical scaling (that is, resources increase) and horizontal scaling (instance count increase) [8] and an algorithm that adapts to different applications and resource usage patterns is proposed.

The SWITCH architecture consists of a load balancer to distribute the requests between the application instances, two monitoring mechanisms (container-level monitoring agent and application-level monitoring agent), a time series database, an alerting mechanism, and an adapting component that responds to such alerts. Additionally, a graphic user interface to configure thresholds and analyzing events is included.

Based on the metrics collected by the monitoring agents, both horizontal scaling (more containers) and vertical scaling (more resources in the same node) is performed.

As for the technologies mentioned in the article, the load balancer is HAProxy[4], the database is Apache Cassandra[5], and the monitoring, alerting and adapting component are developed in Java[6].

2.2 COCOS

Meanwhile, the COCOS architecture assumes that the monitoring part is already solved and it focuses on the control of containers. It has three control levels: container level [8], virtual machine level and cluster level [9].

In order to scale the containers, application metrics (response times, workload) that come from the containers themselves are used. The latter can also have Adaptation Hooks, code portions that allow the application to respond to scaling taking advantage of the new resources (for instance, increasing the thread count).

At the virtual machine level, there is a Supervisor for every one of the machines that handles the resource requests from containers (vertical scaling) and communicates with the next level in order to coordinate container scaling.

Lastly, at the cluster level there is an Orchestrator that manages the horizontal scaling of the containers (that is, the creation of new instances of containers and virtual machines).

2.3 Lightweight Kubernetes Distributions

Some lightweight Kubernetes distributions worth mentioning are micro k8s, k3s and k0s. All of them provide an easy way to run a Kubernetes cluster in a lightweight form. The main goal of them is to provide a solution that can run on a laptop or PC with a small set of resources. One of its main disadvantages is that understanding the technical

---

[4] http://www.haproxy.org/.
[5] https://cassandra.apache.org/_/index.htm.
[6] https://www.java.com.

aspects for its implementation can be a bit challenging for a user who is starting in the technology. All of them require important knowledge in writing YAML files or manifests which determine how applications should be run on clusters.

Micro k8s was designed to be a production-ready lightweight Kubernetes distribution, and it can run on any operating system. Installing MicroK8s is easy on Linux distributions and a bit difficult on Windows and macOS. One nice feature of MicroK8s is that it automatically configures your cluster to be highly available. On the other hand, because of its modular and minimalist design, it only runs a minimal set of services by default, thus results in the need to manually activate services if required.

k3s is another lightweight Kubernetes distribution developed by Rancher. It can also run on any operating system (Linux, Windows, and macOS). It is relatively easy to set up and it has a production grade level.

k0s is the easiest of the three Kubernetes distributions to install, although it only runs in Linux, and runs in an experimental mode on Windows. It is an Open Source initiative distributed under the Apache 2 license, and was developed as a single binary file that encapsulates all the dependencies needed by the distribution.

There are many other Kubernetes distributions, but the main characteristic of all of them is that despite being light, they maintain the need to have a relative amount of resources for their execution.

3   Design Evolution of Crane

DEHIA is a workflow manager for human-intervened data collection [10]. Its architecture is based on microservices. In a first delivery attempt at a local server, it proved to be complex and hard to replicate because of its various components and technologies.

A possible solution to this problem is containerization [8]. The simplest component, a gateway, was chosen to start. This component has no functional dependencies to the other components and it has no internal state.

The gateway component only needs one open port (in order to receive the requests it has to redirect) and it expects a small set of parameters. Because of that, it was viable to deploy it automatically. For this purpose it was decided to develop an automatic Docker deployment tool (named "Crane"), with the addition of scaling the application on-demand creating new instances.

3.1   Instances Load Balancing

Crane must be capable of interacting directly with the container platform, so that a first version was developed as a console script (bash, specifically) that uses Docker commands.

As a consequence of the new instance creation feature, it was necessary to add a load balancer that would make transparent the use of the component. For this purpose, a HTTP proxy (NGINX[7]) with load balancing capabilities, was used.

For portability and ease of use reasons, it was decided to use and configure the containerized version of the proxy. That way, this version of the tool is capable of

---

[7] https://nginx.org/en/.

creating not only instances, but also the proxy itself, configured for each component. NGINX was used because it communicates via HTTP. However, this restricts the tool to applications that share this feature. In addition to that, the application must be load-balancing-compatible (by having separate persistence means, by synchronizing them or not having them).

Inside the same script, an internal network is created for the containers to communicate with each other, leaving outbound access to the load balancer entrance. Figure 1 shows this version of the tool, in which a console script (bash) interacts directly with Docker through console commands.

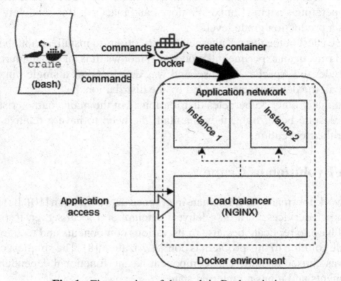

Fig. 1. First version of the tool, in Bash scripting

In Fig. 1, the Docker actions (black filled arrow), as a result of the commands sent by the script (simple arrow), create each of the containers inside the Docker environment, that is, the Load Balancer and the Instances.

Crane also interacts directly with the load balancer in order to notify it about the new instances created (also with a simple arrow) and that way directs correctly the requests that come from the outside (white filled arrow).

Inside the Docker environment, the load balancer allows access to both instances in a transparent way (dashed-line arrow).

Lastly, all the application containers belong to the same network (in a dashed-line square). This means that it could be multiple applications, each running in its own network and isolated from the others.

In order to modify the configuration of the load balancer each time an instance is created, a small script written in Python that waits for configuration updates was added. This updates are sent by the script itself via HTTP (specifically with the curl[8] command,

---

[8] https://curl.se/.

a library and application for this purpose) and they affect the proxy configuration when it reloads as part of the script.

In short, to this point there is a console script that starts with three parameters: the name of the Docker image to be instantiated, the port where it must listen, and the container start parameters. When it starts, the container creates the following elements:

- An inter-container network [11] where only the containers related to the application (instances and load balancer) will be connected.
- The first instance of the application, connected to the aforementioned network, but with no external access.
- The load balancer, configured to direct all the requests to the first instance. The Docker image of the load balancer was modified in order to receive the network location of the first instance as a parameter, and it also includes the Python script previously mentioned. It has two external access points: the application port that was received as a parameter by the console script, and the configuration port that waits for scaling instructions.

Table 1 shows each startup option for the script.

Table 1. Startup options for the Bash version of Crane

Option	Description
Start (image, port, parameters)	It creates a inter-container network, the first instance of the application and the preconfigured load balancer
Scale (identifier)	It creates a new instance of the application and configures the load balancer via HTTP
Descale (identifier, instance)	It deletes the indicated instance and reconfigures the load balancer via HTTP

3.2 Container Automatic Scaling

Scaling this way is not practical because of two reasons: firstly, the administrator must decide when to scale in a manual way. Secondly, there are no metrics for the administrator to make such a decision.

Because of that, it was decided to make a second version of Crane that would scale automatically with an approximated rule (which is not in scope of this work) and that would also employ application use metrics in order to make the decision.

At this point it's interesting to notice that there are two types of use metrics [6]: 1- application metrics, including request count and response times, and others, and 2- infrastructure metrics, including CPU, memory, storage and network usage levels, and others.

For the first case, it can be measured by taking information in the application itself or at the load balancer, and it can be improved by scaling the application. For the second case, it can be measured by asking Docker or the operative system for information, and it can be improved by scaling resources (thinking of a virtual machine with elastic provisioning of CPU and memory).

As Crane is designed for local deployment in a personal computer, and there is no way of automatically increasing the resources, infrastructure metrics will not be considered.

To the moment, there wasn't a mechanism to collect application metrics, and because of that after researching the features of NGINX a module[9] was found. This module allows to keep track of the metrics that could be of interest for the tool (connection count, response times). Then, a new Docker image for the load balancer was designed. This image compiles NGINX with the nginx-module-vts module and includes the Python remote configuration script. In addition to that, the module was configured to listen in a third port (being the first one the access to the application and the second one the remote configuration) from where it returns the aforementioned metrics.

For the second part, that is, to have an approximated rule based in metrics from the load balancer in order to know when to scale, the following condition was set up: "when the sum of the average per second (rate) of the request count received in the last five minutes exceeds the value 0.1". This threshold set on 0.1, and also the five-minute window, are empirical values that allow for a high but manually achievable request rate to trigger the scaling (so it can be noticed).

This condition is useful when the right tool is available. This tool would, on one hand, keep track of the historical requests and, on the other hand, detect when the mentioned condition is met.

Prometheus and Alertmanager. In order to implement this automatic scaling, Prometheus[10], a time series database was used. This means that its specific functionality is to keep track of historical data in order to calculate statistics. On the other hand, it allows to set up alerts that are triggered when a particular condition is met. This "triggered" state implies that the alert is on the alert list in the "firing" state (active).

Prometheus has an external module called Alertmanager[11] whose purpose is to detect the alerts emitted by Prometheus and then trigger notifications through several mechanisms, of which the "webhooks" one is of interest.

A webhook is a URL, provided by the side interested in the alert, where it waits for an Alertmanager notification. This mechanism implies that the URL, that in this case would belong to the console deployment script, must be accessible by Alertmanager. In order to take advantage of using Alertmanager it was noticed that the script would need server capacities in order to receive the alerts, which makes the tool more complex. Figure 2 shows the message sequence between the components that lead to the scaling of a container.

3.3 Detected Implementation Problems

When adding Prometheus and Alertmanager, a set of problems were detected, and that led to rethink the design of Crane from scratch.

---

[9] https://github.com/vozlt/nginx-module-vts.

[10] https://prometheus.io/.

[11] https://prometheus.io/docs/alerting/latest/alertmanager/.

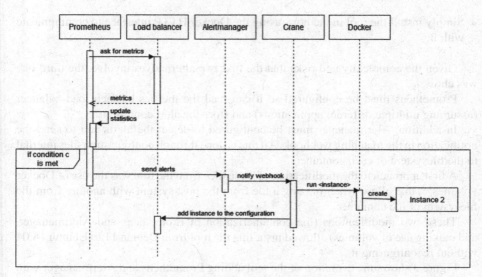

Fig. 2. Automatic instance creation process

Portability Between Installations. The difficulty level of reinstalling the full tool was considered.

Install the tool in another installation of the same operative system (Debian 11) or a Linux system with bash installed used to take just copying the scripts and installing Docker.

However, adding Prometheus and Alertmanager implies installing and configuring them, which is not trivial. One way to automate the configuration is to use the containerized versions of both tools, preconfigured to be instantiated by the script automatically. This led to an apparent conflict with the use of webhooks: if the tool is installed in the host system and Alertmanager is installed inside a container, the latter cannot send the notification because Docker containers have no access to the host system ports.

After more detailed research, it was found that from Docker version 20.10 (end of 2020) this is possible using a special DNS name and the –add-host parameter [12], so that the idea of containerize the module could continue.

For most of the components the containerized version was used, except the console script, which has to interact with Docker in the host system. Three alternatives were considered [13]:

- Docker-outside-of-Docker: it involves sharing the Docker socket with a container that has permissions on it. In this way Docker can be manipulated directly from a container. As the socket requires administrator rights on the host, it is a risky alternative.
- Docker-in-Docker [14]: it involves running Docker inside a container that generates another container inside itself. For this to work, the main container has to be in "privileged mode" (with administrator rights), which could also lead to one of the containerized applications to take control of the local host. Minikube uses this approach.

- Simply install the tool in the host, using the Docker HTTP interface to communicate with it.

Given the complexity and risks that the first two alternatives involve, the third one was chosen.

Prometheus must be configured so it can read the metrics of each load balancer (assuming multiple different applications) and store the alert condition.

In addition, Alertmanager must be configured to detect the alerts and to send the notification in the matching webhook. All this is done through configuration files internal to the filesystem of each container.

A first approach to the modification of these files from the tool was the use of Docker volumes[12], that allow synchronizing a file from the host system with another from the filesystem of the container.

These two modifications (the containerization of Prometheus and Alertmanager, and making use of volumes) allowed installing the tool from Debian 11 to Ubuntu 18.04 without reconfiguring it.

Figure 3 shows the evolution of the tool adding Prometheus and Alertmanager with their respective volumes.

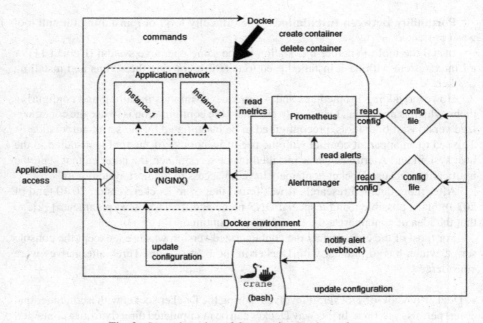

Fig. 3. Second version of Crane using Docker volumes

It can be noticed how the volumes require the files to be outside of the Docker environment and, because of that, they have access to the host filesystem.

---

[12] https://docs.docker.com/storage/volumes/.

Portability between different operating systems. It is of interest to increase the portability of the tool, taking advantage of Docker's multiplatform feature.

Two problems were considered: 1- bash console scripts are not instantly compatible with other systems like Windows (although there is a Linux subsystem, the intent was not to depend on the console) and 2- Docker volumes depend on the filesystem. Even when all major operating systems supporting Docker also support volumes, they are not necessarily compatible[13].

The first problem was solved in two steps: first, the tool was migrated to use the Docker HTTP interface[14] through curl in the console. This decoupled the commands given to Docker from console commands. In a second step, the Python Docker SDK was used. This involved rewriting the tool in Python, which is multiplatform. At the moment the tool requires installing a Python interpreter, which although portable requires configuration and installing libraries. By using Cython[15], a Python extension for C language, a small self-contained executable can be generated.

This new version of the tool makes use of Flask[16], a minimalistic framework form web application development. The console format was abandoned for a REST service that allows (via HTTP) both creating "components" (each one a containerized application) from the same parameters that the previous version (image, port and parameters), and receiving Alertmanager alerts. In order to do that, an object model that considers container images, instances and other managed containers (Prometheus and Alertmanager) was adopted. A self-contained SQLite[17] database was also added. The SQLalchemy[18] ORM was used to map classes to tables. Figure 4 shows the classes model of the tool.

Even when using files generally brings compatibility problems, sharing the file between installations is not planned.

Figure 4 shows the classes for the components, their instances and the class for the managed containers, that is used to clean all the containers (instances, load balancer, Prometheus, Alertmanager) when closing or restarting the application.

The second problem, related to volumes, was solved by deleting them and opening an HTTP interface that receives configuration messages. This interface consists of a Python script which also uses Flask. That way, the file modifying mechanism becomes encapsulated in the container, and the communication is carried out through a standard mechanism such as HTTP.

Course of Action in Case of an Alert. In case of an alert, the course of action is fixed: add a container. It was considered that it would be desirable to be able to describe, in a policy form, which is the action to take in case of an alert. Multiple alerts can also be considered, some for scaling and other for down-scaling.

For instance, it could be defined that if the condition mentioned in the previous sections ("when the sum of the average per second (rate) of the request count received

---

[13] Since 2019 Kubernetes address this problem by adopting the CSI standard, which presents an unified API for the volume storage.

[14] https://docs.docker.com/engine/api/.

[15] https://cython.org/.

[16] https://flask.palletsprojects.com/en/2.0.x/.

[17] https://www.sqlite.org/index.html.

[18] https://www.sqlalchemy.org/.

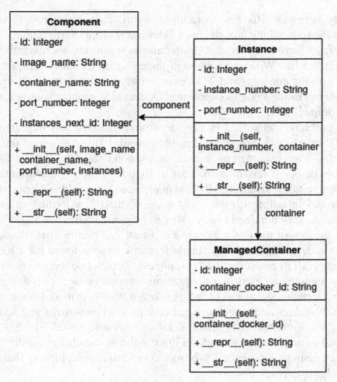

Fig. 4. Object model of the tool (Python version)

in the last five minutes exceeds the value 0.1") a container will be added, but if the threshold is reached in less than two minutes two containers could be added. It also could be defined that if the value is below a certain threshold (0.1, for instance) for a certain time (five minutes, for instance), a container will be removed (if there is more than one). An interesting point is which the selection criteria are when a container has to be deleted. In this case, for simplicity's sake, the oldest container is deleted.

In order to achieve this, a policy management tool called Open Policy Agent[19] was added. It consists of a server capable of making decisions based on an input, a policy and stored data related to a topic. In this case the topic is "actions to perform when an alert fires" and the data is pairs of "alert – action". The actions have the format *[direction] [count]*. For instance, if it is desired to scale up in three containers, the action would take the form *upscale 3*. If the desired behavior is to reduce in one container the total count when other alert fires, the action would be *downscale 1*. The policy simply extracts the action according to the input, which is an alert name.

Difficulty of Use. Given that the tool became a web server, in order to access its functionality it is needed to make HTTP requests to its REST interface. There are three ways to achieve this: 1- Using curl from the console, 2- Using an HTTP client with

---

[19] http://openpolicyagent.org/.

graphic user interface as Postman[20] o 3- Writing a client and integrating it in another system.

The third alternative was chosen and it was decided to develop a graphic user interface in React[21], which allows access to the functionality provided by the tool, and it loads at the same time the alerts in Prometheus and their respective actions in Open Policy Agent. This decision is due to the first alternative going back to the console format, which is rudimentary and the format to avoid, and the second one requiring external tools and extended knowledge of the REST interface of the tool. However, the tool allows any of the three alternatives, and, in fact, a second graphical interface with different requirements could be developed using the same tool. Figure 5 shows a new version that includes a graphic user interface and it leaves out Docker volumes for the Prometheus and Alertmanager configuration.

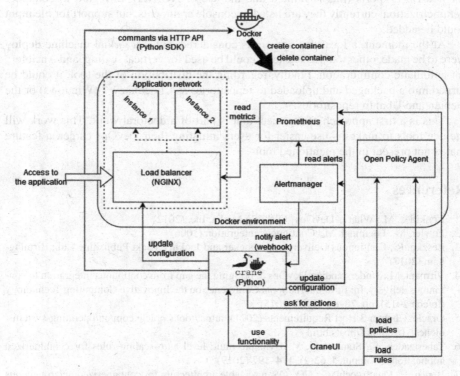

Fig. 5. Third version of Crane with graphical user interface

In this version, the responsibility to load the rules and policies moves to the graphical interface, which uses the functionality of the Python service through its HTTP interface. It can be seen how the configuration update (arrow from Crane Python to Prometheus

---

[20] https://www.postman.com/.

[21] https://reactjs.org/.

and Alert manager) is made directly to the container, which has a small service listening, and not through files, which used to tie the implementation to the operative system.

4   Conclusions and Future Work

A tool for creating containers automatically was presented. It adds load balancing and automatic scaling with configurable rules. Even though it is not in scope of this work, the construction of said rules were thoroughly studied for several application styles by other authors, as in [6].

An interesting point to extend is the possibility of extending the capacities of the tool in order to add automatic deployment of new versions of the Docker images.

In addition, it could add support for multiple ports for each container, or the support for non-HTTP ports (this is limited due the use of NGINX). In regard to container parametrization, currently they are listed as console arguments, but support for file input could be added.

At the moment, a local deployment is considered, but if a virtual machine deploy were to be made, other tools as Packer[22] could be used for vertical scaling, and Ansible[23] for automatic configuration. Finally, regarding the distribution of the tool, it could be turned into a packaged and uploaded to repositories as Chocolatey[24] (Windows) or the Debian and Ubuntu repositories.

This is a first approach of a project that is part of a doctoral work. This work will include tools to make its use easier for users initiating their DevOps career, a feature that is not present in the mentioned tools.

References

1. Loukides, M.: What is DevOps? O'Reilly Media, Inc. (2012)
2. Fowler, M., Foemmel, M.: Continuous integration (2006)
3. Leszko, R.: Continuous Delivery with Docker and Jenkins. Packt Publishing Ltd., Birmingham (2017)
4. Virmani, M.: Understanding DevOps & bridging the gap from continuous integration to continuous delivery. In: Fifth International Conference on the Innovative Computing Technology (intech 2015), pp. 78–82. IEEE (2015)
5. Oracle: Chapter 3 Host Requirements (2021). https://docs.oracle.com/en/operating-systems/olcne/1.1/relnotes/hosts.html
6. Taherizadeh, S., Stankovski, V.: Dynamic multi-level auto-scaling rules for containerized applications. Comput. J. **62**(2), 174–197 (2019)
7. Baresi, L., Quattrocchi, G.: COCOS: a scalable architecture for containerized heterogeneous systems. In: 2020 IEEE International Conference on Software Architecture (ICSA), pp. 103–113. IEEE (2020)
8. Bullington-McGuire, R., Dennis, A.K., Schwartz, M.: Docker for developers: develop and run your application with Docker containers using DevOps tools for continuous delivery. Packt Publishing (2020)

---

[22] https://www.packer.io/.
[23] https://www.ansible.com/.
[24] https://chocolatey.org/.

9. Erl, T., Puttini, R., Mahmood, Z.: Cloud computing: concepts, technology, & architecture. Pearson Education (2013)
10. Arcidiacono: DEHIA: una plataforma liviana para definir y ejecutar actividades con intervención humana basadas en workflows (*DEHIA: a lightweight platform to define and execute human intervention activities based on workflows*). Degree thesis. Facultad de Informática, UNLP (2020)
11. Docker: Networking with standalone containers (2022). https://docs.docker.com/network/network-tutorial-standalone/
12. Docker: Docker Engine release notes (2020). https://docs.docker.com/engine/release-notes/#20100
13. Nestybox: Secure Docker-in-Docker with System Containers (2019). https://blog.nestybox.com/2019/09/14/dind.html
14. Docker: Docker can now run within Docker (2013). https://www.docker.com/blog/docker-can-now-run-within-docker

Machine and Deep Learning

Multi-class E-mail Classification with a Semi-Supervised Approach Based on Automatic Feature Selection and Information Retrieval

Juan Manuel Fernández[1]([✉]) [iD] and Marcelo Errecalde[2] [iD]

[1] Department of Basic Sciences, National University of Lujan, Lujan, Argentina
jmfernandez@unlu.edu.ar
[2] LIDIC, National University of San Luis, San Luis, Argentina
merreca@unsl.edu.ar

Abstract. Nowadays, millions of data are generated every day, and their use and interpretation have become fundamental in all fields. This is particularly true in the area of e-mails classification where, beyond its key role in organizing huge amounts of incoming information, it presents several challenging aspects to be solved. To the well-known problems presented by textual data (as its ambiguity) e-mails are usually characterized by their short lenght and informal language. These difficulties are increased when a relatively large number of highly imbalanced classes need to be considered and manual labeling is expensive and must be carried out by specialized personnel. Those are the main issues addressed in the present work, where Spanish-language e-mails sent by students of an Argentinian university needs to be categorized in 16 different classes.

Our proposal to address this problem consists of a semi-supervised approach based on an automatic feature selection process complemented with an information retrieval strategy. From an initial data set of manually labeled e-mails, the main features are selected for each class, using three techniques: logistic regression, TF-IDF, and SS3. Then, the remaining (non labeled) instances are indexed with a general-purpose search engine (Elasticsearch) and documents of each class are retrieved based on the selected features identified by each technique.

Our very simple approach shows that classifiers trained with labeled documents plus those retrieved in an automatic way obtain an improvement in performance (up to 6%) regarding classifiers trained only with manually labeled instances. Those improvements are observed in both, traditional learning algorithms like SVM, but also in more recent, state of the arts, transformer-based models (BERT).

Keywords: Semi-supervised text classification · Feature selection · Multi-class unbalanced data

© The Author(s), under exclusive license to Springer Nature Switzerland AG 2022
E. Rucci et al. (Eds.): JCC-BD&ET 2022, CCIS 1634, pp. 75–90, 2022.
https://doi.org/10.1007/978-3-031-14599-5_6

1   Introduction

As a result of the overcrowding of Internet access, millions and millions of data are generated every day and their exploitation and interpretation have become fundamental in all areas. As an example, the increasing number of e-mails that people and organizations receive on a daily base, have posed the need of tools to automatically organize them, a research area known as *email mining* [3]. Email is one of the most widespread asynchronous communication tools today. It has displaced the more classical communication channels due to its high efficiency, extremely low cost, and compatibility with many different types of information. With more than 3930 million of e-mail users worldwide and a current traffic of 293.6 billion emails sent daily [12,26], this medium has become a standard communication channel not only for regular people but also for public and private contact centers. There, huge amount of e-mails are received requiring significant human resources to process them. For instance, answering a citizen's email sent to the Swedish Pension Agency takes about 10 min and, therefore, the 99,000 messages they receive per year may require up to 10 full-time employees to answer them [25].

When knowledge extraction from e-mails is only focussed on their content parts (text), different text mining techniques have been applied that exclusively relies on textual databases as data sources [28]. These techniques have to face typical difficulties of language analysis (derived from its ambiguity) which are increased when the e-mails contain informal (noisy) language and the length of texts is relatively short. Short and informal texts present challenging scenarios to text mining in general, and text classification in particular [21]. These problems are aggravated when there are few labeled training instances available and the number of classes is high with a notable imbalance in their sizes [7].

In the present work, we address a scenario that presents those challenging aspects in a real-world problem of e-mails classification in an Argentinian University. There, hundreds of (informal) e-mails sent by the students need to be classified according to the type of question the student asked. The administrative staff has available thousands of e-mails but only a few are labeled with the right type of question. In that context, learning of a supervised classifier model presents additional difficulties due to a relatively high number of imbalanced classes. Our proposal to deal with this problem is a novel and simple semi-supervised approach that combines automatic feature selection of the representative words of each class with a strategy for e-mails retrieval of each class using the ElasticSearch tool.

Experimental results show that enriching labeled instances with automatically labeled e-mails allows improving (in up to 6%) results obtained only with labeled data not only with traditional learning algorithms like SVM but also with more recent, state of the arts (deep learning) transformer-based models like BERT.

The rest of the article is organized as follows. Section 2 presents some related works, the research gap addressed in this article and our working hypotesis. Section 3 presents the research methodology with its involved tasks and Sect. 4

describes the experimental study and the analysis of the results. Finally, Sect. 5 gives some general conclusions, contributions of our work and identifies possible lines of future work.

2 Background

In full-scale machine learning applications, it is usual to have available abundant unlabeled training examples but few reliable labeled instances. Labeling those examples can require a lot of human effort mainly when is to be done by people specialized in the problem domain. As a consequence, *semi-supervised learning* in general, and *semi-supervised classification* in particular has generated a lot of attention in the last times [29]. As the name suggests, the concept of semi-supervised learning lies between supervised and unsupervised learning. Most semi-supervised learning strategies rely on extending supervised or unsupervised learning to include additional information typical of the other learning paradigm.

Formally, given a labeled dataset $D_l = \{(x_i, y_i) | (x_i, y_i) \in X \times Y, i = 1, ..., l\}$, and an unlabeled dataset $D_u = \{x_j | x_j \in X, j = l + 1, ..., l + u\}$, where X comprises the feature space of the instances and Y labels or classes, a semi-supervised algorithm aims to train a classifier f from $D_l \cup D_u$, that is, from the labeled and unlabeled data, in such a way that it performance is better than the supervised classifier trained only with the labeled data [23,31].

In this context, different strategies for the semi-supervised classification of documents have been studied and developed to provide greater scalability [20]. In some mass-use systems, one possible strategy is to infer implicit labels from the behavior of the people who use the system. However, this requires large populations of users to be consolidated, as in the case of Internet search engines [15].

An alternative approach to data labeling consists of "distant supervision", in which the training data are labeled based on some text features, such as tags, emoticons, and other metadata [11]. This interesting approach have obtained good results in social networks where some emoticons can be indicators of user's sentiment. Those symbols have the advantage of being independent of the domain, their topics and time [19].

When it is neccesary to learn from positive and unlabeled examples, the semi-supervised method "PU-Learning" has shown its effectivenes in differet works [9,10]. In this case, a set of documents of a particular topic or class P (positive class) is complemented by a subset of mixed documents that do not correspond to a specific class. The idea here is, from the iterative construction of a group of classifiers identifying a set of reliable negative documents from the unlabeled set.

In multi-class problems, one approach that has shown promising results instead of labeling a set of documents, proposes labeling a set of *representative words* of each class and then automatically labeling a set of documents based on the presence of those representative words [17]. The key of this approach is to choose a set of *truly representative* words for each class. In that process, although the user is assisted in selecting those words, the final election of the representative words is carried out manually by the user. That differs with our proposal in the present work, where the representative words of each class are automatically selected by different methods.

Moreover, here in time, one can observe works using feature extraction and clustering with K-Means for semi-supervised labeling of emails [1,13,18]. While these works address sentiment analysis, which faces different challenges to the multi-label classification addressed in this work, there are parallels in the processes of document corpus preprocessing and the feature selection strategies used to represent feelings.

It is important to note, that most of the previous works address the problem known as sentiment/polarity analysis, where classes generally have two states, making it feasible to intensify the position to predict one of them and determine the other from the complement of the first one. This approach allows, usually through clustering techniques, to find similarities between documents of the same class. We can hypothesize, that similar semi-supervised approaches might be also useful in other (binary) e-mail classification tasks such as spam detection.

The problem addressed in the present work differs from the above ones in considering a relatively large number (16) of highly unbalanced classes, a setting that, as far as we know, not have been frequently analyzed in the e-mail classification area. Our working hypothesis is that a simple methodology of automatic selection of representative features of each class combined with adequated information retrieval approaches constitutes a valid and simple semi-supervised method for the automatic classification of e-mails in multi-class, highly imbalanced settings. In this context, it is verified that the results obtained with the models trained by this approach show a considerable improvement on those obtained only with manually labeled data.

3   Research Methodology

As discussed above, the overall objective of this research is to generate a process for semi-supervised document classification on a case study based on Spanish language e-mails by identifying key features of each class using feature selection techniques and then retrieving e-mails automatically using an information retrieval approach. Figure 1 illustrates the workflow developed in the framework of this article.

Initially, starting from an initial collection of manually labeled e-mails, each class's main features were extracted using three techniques: logistic regression, TF-IDF, and SS3. Then, the remaining e-mails are indexed with a general-purpose search engine such as *Elasticsearch*, and documents of each class are retrieved based on the features detected by each technique. The classifier trained with those data, is finally evaluated with a previously separated test set. This process comprises several sub-task in the different stages like the preprocessing of e-mails before the manual labeling, the use of three feature extraction strategies, the retrieval and labeling of documents based on those features with a search

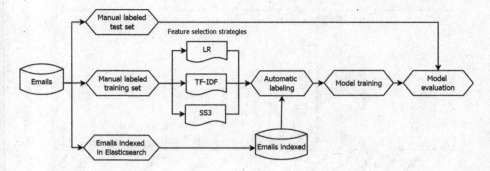

Fig. 1. Workflow for semi-supervised labeling of emails

engine, and the construction of a classification model and its comparison against the models generated without the use of this process.

3.1   Description of the Dataset

For the experiments, we used a collection of 24700 e-mails generated from academic questions made by students to the administrative staff of the National University of Lujan. These questions are about procedures derived from the academic activity and the original e-mails were used without fixing any kind of typos or syntax errors.

3.2   Labeling of Documents

From those 24700 e-mails, 1000 were randomly selected and labeled around the question topic by a domain expert. Each class represents a particular kind of question that students usually ask to the administrative personnel of the university. The frequency distribution for each class is shown in Fig. 2.

The 16 classes, all independent of each other, resulting from the labeling are: *Boleto Universitario, Cambio de Carrera, Cambio de Comisión, Consulta por Equivalencias, Consulta por Legajo, Consulta sobre Título Universitario, Cursadas, Datos Personales, Exámenes, Ingreso a la Universidad, Pedido de Certificados, Problemas con la Clave, Reincorporación, Requisitos de Ingreso, Simultaneidad de Carreras y Situación Académica.* As it can be seen, the classes are highly unbalanced, an aspect that usually difficulties the classification process and that will be addressed with the process proposed in this paper.

3.3   Email Indexing

Elasticsearch is a free and open distributed search and analysis engine that allows storing and indexing multiple types of data, including textual, numerical, geospatial, structured, and unstructured[1]. Elasticsearch supports text in 34

---

[1] Taken from https://www.elastic.co/es/what-is/elasticsearch.

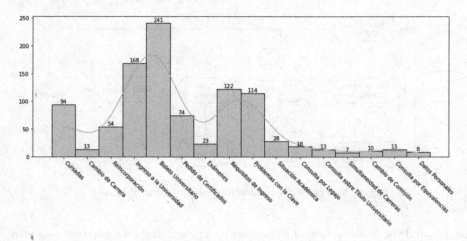

Fig. 2. Observed frequency for classes resulting from manual labeling

different languages and provides analyzers for each language. The analyzers are composed of a chain of filters that perform transformations on the texts to be indexed, so that the transformations performed by each analyzer depend on the filters it uses. For this research, all the emails were indexed in an instance of Elasticsearch and the standard analyzer for the Spanish language was applied.

3.4 Feature Selection Strategies

Before the application of feature selection strategies, the text was converted to lowercase, stopwords were removed, and different variations of word n-grams were experimented with. As feature selection strategies, we used the coefficients learned by a logistic regression algorithm for each class, the TF-IDF weighting grouped by classes and the word rating obtained with the Sequential S3 (Smoothness, Significance, and Sanction) or simply SS3. Below, a brief synopsis of those techniques is given.

TF-IDF. One of the best-known term weighting methods is TF-IDF (term frequency-inverse document frequency) which is formed from two more basic metrics: TF and IDF. TF (term frequency) captures the importance (number of ocurrences) of a term for a document. IDF reflects the importance of a term for a document in a corpus of documents [27]. Indeed, this relationship allows the TF-IDF value to increase proportionally to the number of times a term appears in a document, but to be penalized if that term appears too frequently in the remaining documents [2]. In the context of this research, this weighting, grouped by class, is used to determine the essential terms for each class.

SS3. It is an incremental text classification technique that has shown be effective in early risk detection problems [4]. This technique allows to be used for feature extraction since it generates a function $gv(w, c)$ that values words in relation to categories; to be more specific, gv takes a word w and a category c and generates a number in the interval $[0,1]$ that represents the degree of confidence with which w belongs exclusively to c.

Logistic Regression. It is a probabilistic statistical classification technique. It is used as a binary model to predict a binary response or the outcome of a categorical or discrete dependent variable as a function of one or more variables [14]. This function is helpful since, for any real numerical input, it generates an output restricted to values between 0 and 1 and, therefore, can be interpreted as a probability. In turn, it is adapted to problems with non-binary responses where, intuitively, the way to approach these problems is to differentiate one class from the rest successive times, determining a different function for each of them [24]. In this work, we use the coefficients generated by the function of each class for the extraction of the most representative terms.

Feature selection was performed from a training dataset, which consisted of 800 out of the 1000 instances manually labeled by an expert. The remaining 200 were reserved for model evaluations. From these training instances, the previously presented strategies were run.

In the case of TF-IDF, it was introduced as an unsupervised term weighting strategy and applied in conjunction with a vector-based document-representation or bag-of-words model [22]. The terms were weighted with TF-IDF[2] for each term in each document, then grouped by class, leaving a matrix with the classes as instances and the terms (with their TF-IDF weighting) as columns. To select the most representative terms for each class, we chose to select the 20 terms with the highest average TF-IDF weighting per class. Figure 3 presents all the representative terms of the class 'Problems with the Key' in a wordcloud graph, according to the TF-IDF and SS3 strategies, without limiting the number of terms.

SS3 is incorporated as a supervised feature selection strategy since this technique generates a vocabulary for each class with a weighting based on a confidence value or CV. In this case, a classification model was fitted with SS3 for the 800 training instances, and the terms corresponding to the vocabulary of each class were obtained, using the 20 most representative ones.

Finally, logistic regression is another supervised strategy that allows to identify, in addition to the representative terms for each class, a set of terms that are harmful to the choice of a given topic. In this case, documents represented in the vector model are used to train a model[3] with the training instances and the 10 terms with the highest weights -in absolute value- were selected for both positive and negative examples.

---

[2] For this purpose, the default TF-IDF formula of the *TfidfVectorizer* class of the *sklearn* Python library was used.

[3] Previously, a grid search was performed alternating different values of the parameter C of the Logistic Regression class of the **sklearn** library, varying the weighting schemes of the terms. The best value was obtained with $C = 1$.

Fig. 3. Representative terms for the class 'Problemas con la clave' (SS3 & TF-IDF)

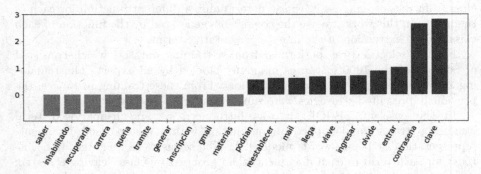

Fig. 4. Weights of the terms obtained with Logistic Regression for the class 'Problemas con la Clave'

3.5 Retrieval of E-mails

Based on the most representative terms for each class -and their weighting-according to the above three feature selection techniques, we retrieved the e-mails indexed in the search engine *Elasticsearch* from two different strategies. On the one hand, a retrieval was made from terms for each class according to their occurrence or not, as a conventional query. On the other hand, we incorporated the weighting of each term according to the different strategies, which is called boosting in the context of the tool. In turn, for the strategy based on logistic regression, a negative nurturing was performed for the terms with coefficients less than zero, penalizing the documents in which they appear. Experiments were performed with batches of 20, 50, 100, and 200 documents for each class and each strategy. It is important to note that the search engine, in addition to the possibility of limiting the number of results, provides a score to magnify the level of similarity of the search in relation to each retrieved document.

For explanatory purposes, Table 1 presents a summary for the logistic regression strategy of the retrieval of 200 documents per class, comparing both document retrieval strategies and a summary of the scores obtained in each class in terms of similarity concerning each other. In this sense, the columns Coincidences (Coinc.) and Differences (Diff.) columns show the number of matched and divergent retrieved emails concerning the retrieval strategies with and without boosting, while the remaining columns are shown as a summary in terms of the scores assigned by the Elasticsearch tool for each class.

Table 1. Retrieval with *Elasticsearch* (doc = 200) with and without sin boosting (LR)

Class	Coinc.	Diff.	Max	Min	Avg
Boleto Universitario	141	59	23.22	12.10	14.21
Cambio de Carrera	138	62	14.99	7.62	9.09
Cambio de Comisión	156	44	20.10	8.38	10.52
Equivalencias	143	57	13.11	6.58	8.04
Consulta por Legajo	194	6	19.61	8.64	11.15
Título Universitario	149	51	16.71	7.59	9.28
Cursadas	162	38	13.45	8.04	9.25
Datos Personales	156	44	14.83	6.61	8.27
Exámenes	144	56	19.29	8.61	10.49
Ingreso a la Universidad	176	24	15.00	8.04	9.62
Pedido de Certificados	161	39	28.98	10.57	14.20
Problemas con la Clave	173	27	22.30	8.96	11.16
Reincorporación	147	53	14.25	7.38	8.96
Requisitos de Ingreso	177	23	18.33	10.87	12.86
Simultaneidad	131	69	21.09	7.89	10.34
Situación Académica	125	75	17.53	8.95	11.07
General	**2473**	**727**	**28.98**	**6.58**	**10.53**

3.6   Generation of the Classification Models

At the first time, we used as a training set the instances retrieved for each class from *Elasticsearch* based on the terms generated by each feature selection technique, and then we added the manually labeled instances. In all cases, we compared the performance of the models generated from the presence of automatically labeled documents for the models developed only from the labeled cases.

As for the classification techniques, experiments were carried out with *Support Vector Machines* (SVM) and the *Bidirectional Encoder Representations from Transformer* (BERT) Multiclass Classifier. SVM is one the most robust learning method in the NLP area when combined with traditional (vector model) representations while BERT has recently become the state of the art method in most of the NLP tasks [16].

SVM is a classical approach that has gained popularity over time due to some attractive features and its empirical performance. The main objective of support vector machines is to select the hyperplane which separates the training instances with a maximum distance criterion [24]. BERT is a recent neural network architecture, simpler and more parallelizable than its predecessors. Based exclusively on attentional mechanisms [30], these ideas led to what is today considered the state of the art in language models called BERT [6]. Synthetically, this framework consists of two steps: initial pre-training and subsequent fine-tuning. During pre-training, the model is trained with unlabeled data on different tasks. Then, for fine-tuning, the BERT model is first initialized with the parameters of the pre-trained model, which are adjusted at this stage using labeled data from the subsequent tasks.

For the training of the models, in the case of BERT, we experimented with a pre-trained native model for the Spanish language [5] and a set of hyperparameters successfully used in a previous work on the same data, due to the processing time required for the search of hyperparameters in this type of models and the vast amount of experiments designed for this research [8]. On the other hand, in the case of SVM, a grid search for the best hyperparameters was used[4].

As for the data used for the training stage, different experiments were designed depending on the combination of the instances retrieved by the feature selection strategies and 800 of the manually labeled ones. To evaluate the models, the remaining 200 manually labeled instances were reserved. Finally, the analysis of the selection of the generated models was performed based on the standard metrics *accuracy*, *precision* and *f1-score*.

4   Experiments

For the experiments, the manually labeled instances as well as those retrieved with the three feature selection strategies for 20, 50, and 100 instances, with and without boosting, were used as training sets.

First, to evaluate the relevance of the instances automatically labeled from the three feature selection techniques, those instances were used to train models that were compared againsts models trained from manually labeled e-mails. The results obtained in terms of accuracy are presented in Table 2.

As we can see, the general performance obtained by training with automatic labeled instances is not as good as the obtained with the manualy labeled ones. Therefore, in a second step, we analyzed whether these defficiencies to represent the knowledge of the classes was consistent in the 16 cases or whether the results varied depending on the classes and the 3 strategies applied. For this purpose, we compared the percentage of instances of each class correctly classifed by each method (the recall) using for the feature selction techniques 100 documents retrieved with boosting per class.

---

[4] The hyperparameters alternated throughout the experiments are C, Gamma, and the kernels used by the algorithm.

Table 2. Results with manual versus automatic labeled instances for different feature selection strategies.

Strategy	Manual labeling	N = 20	N = 100	N = 20 boosting	N = 100 boosting
LR+SVM	0.810	0.510	0.665	0.520	0.665
TF-IDF+SVM	0.810	0.560	0.680	0.550	0.690[a]
SS3+SVM	0.810	0.600	0.655	0.580	0.655
LR+BERT	0.855	0.655	0.610	0.625	0.645
TF-IDF+BERT	0.855	0.650	0.720	0.640	0.720
SS3+BERT	0.855	0.610	0.655	0.715	0.645

[a] With $N = 200$ it shows an accuracy of 0.74 while the rest of the strategies decrease their performance.

From Tables 2 and 3 we can conclude that although the automatic labeling of the training examples is not enough to replace a trained model with manual labeling, it could nourish the model with information that would allow "enriching" the training set conformed by the manually labeled instances to improve the results obtained. In fact, the manual labeling strategy only performed better

Table 3. Recall by class for feature selection strategies and SVM

Class	Manual labeling	LR	TF-IDF	SS3	#
Boleto Universitario	**0.98**	0.88	0.90	0.90	48
Cambio de Carrera	0.50	**1.00**	0.50	**1.00**	2
Cambio de Comisión	0.50	0.50	0.50	0.50	2
Consulta Equivalencias	0.67	0.67	0.67	0.67	3
Consulta por Legajo	0.67	0.33	0.67	0.67	3
Consulta sobre Título	0.33	0.67	**1.00**	0.33	3
Cursadas	**0.89**	0.79	0.63	0.53	19
Datos Personales	0.00	0.50	**1.00**	0.60	2
Exámenes	0.60	0.60	**0.80**	**0.80**	5
Ingreso a la Universidad	**0.76**	0.52	0.36	0.42	33
Pedido de Certificados	0.93	0.93	0.93	0.93	15
Problemas con la Clave	**0.96**	0.65	0.87	0.70	23
Reincorporación	**0.73**	0.36	0.18	0.18	11
Requisitos de Ingreso	**0.67**	0.42	0.62	0.62	24
Simultaneidad	0.00	0.00	0.00	**1.00**	1
Situación Académica	0.50	0.67	**0.83**	**0.83**	6
Average	**0.810**	0.665	0.690	0.650	200

than the other strategies in 6 of the 16 classes, suggesting that feature selection strategies probably capture part of the characteristics of the mails that make up each class. An outstanding point of the results obtained, is that, for all classes where the test dataset has less than ten instances (5% of the total), the models based on automatic document labeling perform as well as or better than those based on manual labeling.

From this evidence, and as a next step, starting from the emails retrieved by class, a voting system was built among the instances retrieved by the feature extraction strategies, consolidating a new training dataset made up of the instances that had been retrieved by at least two of the three strategies for the first 100 results of each class.

Table 4. Experiments from a voting system between LR, TF-IDF and SS3.

Strategy	#	Accuracy	Recall	Precision
$(LR \cap TFIDF) + SVM$	925	0.635	0.635	0.787
$(LR \cap SS3) + SVM$	797	0.685	0.685	0.877
$(SS3 \cap TFIDF) + SVM$	1284	0.680	0.680	0.840
$(LR \cap TFIDF \cap SS3) + SVM$	520	0.615	0.615	0.760
$(LR \cap TFIDF) + BERT$	925	0.680	0.680	0.760
$(LR \cap SS3) + BERT$	797	0.615	0.615	0.647
$(SS3 \cap TFIDF) + BERT$	1284	0.720	0.720	0.827
$(LR \cap TFIDF \cap SS3) + BERT$	520	0.690	0.660	0.716

From the above experiments, uneven results are found with respect to using the feature selection strategies one at a time for obtaining the training instances. However, it is interesting to watch the values observed for some models in terms of the precision metric. This allows us to infer that, although the models generated from the instances labeled with the feature selection strategies do not capture all the variance of the testing instances, but they are very precise in identifying those that classify into certain classes.

Next, it is interesting to verify if these strategies are able to improve the performance of the classification models generated from the manually labeled instances by adding to this training set those labeled automatically from each of the three strategies and the combinations among them. A new batch of experiments was then generated and, this time, the comparison of the models is made from the *accuracy, precision* y *f1-score*.

The instances originally labeled manually by the experts were added to the automatically labeled instances to verify whether this methodology robustly classifies the test cases.

Based on the results observed in the experiments of Table 5, it can be stated that several of the combinations among the feature selection strategies, as well as one of the models generated by them taken separately, contribute to provide

Table 5. Experiments with manually labeled instances (M) added to labeled instances from feature selection strategies

Strategy	Accuracy	F1-score	Precision
$M + SVM$	0.810	0.809	0.829
$M + LR + SVM$	0.795	0.806	0.843
$M + TFIDF + SVM$	0.790	0.797	0.819
$M + SS3 + SVM$	0.790	0.792	0.829
$M + (LR \cap SS3) + SVM$	**0.820**	**0.821**	**0.842**
$M + (LR \cap TFIDF) + SVM$	**0.815**	**0.809**	**0.829**
$M + (SS3 \cap TFIDF) + SVM$	**0.830**	**0.833**	**0.856**
$M + (LR \cap TFIDF \cap SS3) + SVM$	**0.835**	**0.831**	**0.849**
$M + BERT$	0.860	0.847	0.845
$M + LR + BERT$	**0.875**	**0.876**	**0.889**
$M + TFIDF + BERT$	0.825	0.827	0.841
$M + SS3 + BERT$	0.825	0.837	0.868
$M + (LR \cap SS3) + BERT$	**0.890**	**0.887**	**0.893**
$M + (LR \cap TFIDF) + BERT$	**0.870**	**0.867**	**0.874**
$M + (SS3 \cap TFIDF) + BERT$	**0.895**	**0.890**	**0.898**
$M + (LR \cap TFIDF \cap SS3) + BERT$	**0.885**	**0.873**	**0.875**

more variance to the set of instances and better models are obtained than those trained only by the manually labeled instances.

Particularly, the strategy that obtained the best results for the most traditional classification technique, such as support vector machines (SVM), results from the combination of SS3 and TF-IDF, obtaining improvements in terms of all metrics between 2% and 3%. Improvements are also observed for the transformer-based models (BERT), obtaining the best model for the strategy resulting from combining SS3 and TFIDF, with improvements between 4% and 6% for the metrics evaluated.

5   Conclusions

This article presents a novel and simple approach for semi-supervised classification of e-mails in multi-class settings. To validate the proposal, a data set was generated with e-mails from students of an Argentinian University. These e-mails, containing questions about different admistrative and academic aspects were collected, processed and 1000 of them manually labeled by people specialized in the problem domain. This data set is made available for the authors for replication of results and further research on this problem.

The addressed problem is interesting because it has several challenging aspects that we can frequently find in text classification problems in the real world: short and (noisy) informal texts, a relatively large number of (unbalanced) classes and few labeled instances for supervised learning. In that context, it is important to note that the proposal could be used in domains with similar characteristics or e-mails in other languages (beyond the Spanish) because the proposed techniques are quite independent of the used language.

The proposal integrates automatic feature selection strategies and information retrieval tools for automatically classify unlabeled instances for training. In that context, this research investigates the effectiveness of three strategies such as Logistic Regresion, SS3, and TF-IDF for feature selection in texts to implement the proposed semi-supervised classification of emails.

First, it was possible to verify that the three strategies adequately identify the most important terms in the text. At the same time, it is possible to use the weights defined by each technique to evaluate the representativeness of these terms.

Second, it was shown that these feature selection techniques, used as automatic word labeling strategies with an information retrieval approach, allow to improve the capacity of the classifiers when automatically labeled instances are incorporated into the manually labeled ones to train the model. The comparison of the results obtained in each class allows concluding that this improvement is originated by the information that provide automatic labeled instances to detect classes with very few instances.

In particular, it is observed that these strategies are effective when used by combining the instances labeled by more than one feature selection strategy, where all models outperform the models generated by the manually labeled documents.

It is then concluded that selecting representative characteristics of each class from the techniques discussed, combined with information retrieval approaches, constitutes a valid and simple semi-supervised method for the automatic classification of e-mails.

As future work, it is proposed to make adjustments to the offered strategy, both in terms of the selected features techniques and the fine-tuning of the N that identifies the number of representative terms for each class. Another issue to consider is the impact on the calibration of these aspects for the efficiency and efficacy of this strategy.

Finally, for the consolidation of the proposed semi-supervised learning strategy, further empirical tests on other datasets are still pending to ratify its usefulness while helping to identify the most favorable contexts for its use.

References

1. Ali, R.S.H., El Gayar, N.: Sentiment analysis using unlabeled email data. In: 2019 International Conference on Computational Intelligence and Knowledge Economy (ICCIKE), pp. 328–333. IEEE (2019)
2. Bafna, P., Pramod, D., Vaidya, A.: Document clustering: TF-IDF approach. In: 2016 International Conference on Electrical, Electronics, and Optimization Techniques (ICEEOT), pp. 61–66. IEEE (2016)

3. Bogawar, P.S., Bhoyar, K.K.: Email mining: a review. Int. J. Comput. Sci. Issues **9**(1), 429–434 (2012)
4. Burdisso, S.G., Errecalde, M., Montes-y Gómez, M.: A text classification framework for simple and effective early depression detection over social media streams. Expert Syst. Appl. **133**, 182–197 (2019)
5. Cañete, J., Chaperon, G., Fuentes, R., Ho, J.H., Kang, H., Pérez, J.: Spanish pretrained BERT model and evaluation data. In: PML4DC at ICLR 2020 (2020)
6. Devlin, J., Chang, M.W., Lee, K., Toutanova, K.: Bert: pre-training of deep bidirectional transformers for language understanding. arXiv preprint arXiv:1810.04805 (2018)
7. Fernández, A., García, S., Galar, M., Prati, R.C., Krawczyk, B., Herrera, F.: Learning from Imbalanced Data Sets. Springer, Cham (2018). https://doi.org/10.1007/978-3-319-98074-4
8. Fernandez, J.M., Cavasin, N., Errecalde, M.: Classic and recent (neural) approaches to automatic text classification: a comparative study with e-mails in the Spanish language. In: Short Papers of the 9th Conference on Cloud Computing, Big Data & Emerging Topics, p. 20 (2021)
9. Ferretti, E., Errecalde, M.L., Anderka, M., Stein, B.: On the use of reliable-negatives selection strategies in the PU learning approach for quality flaws prediction in Wikipedia. In: 2014 25th International Workshop on Database and Expert Systems Applications, pp. 211–215. IEEE (2014)
10. Ferretti, E., Hernández Fusilier, D., Guzmán Cabrera, R., Montes y Gómez, M., Errecalde, M., Rosso, P.: On the use of PU learning for quality flaw prediction in Wikipedia. In: CEUR Workshop Proceedings, vol. 1178 (2012)
11. Go, A., Bhayani, R., Huang, L.: Twitter sentiment classification using distant supervision. CS224N Proj. Rep. Stanford **1**(12), 2009 (2009)
12. Group, T.R.: Email statistics report, 2019–2023 (2019). http://www.radicati.com
13. Gupta, I., Joshi, N.: Real-time twitter corpus labelling using automatic clustering approach. Int. J. Comput. Digit. Syst. **10**, 519–532 (2021)
14. Igual, L., Seguí, S.: Introduction to data science. In: Introduction to Data Science. UTCS, pp. 1–4. Springer, Cham (2017). https://doi.org/10.1007/978-3-319-50017-1_1
15. Joachims, T.: Optimizing search engines using clickthrough data. In: Proceedings of the Eighth ACM SIGKDD International Conference on Knowledge Discovery and Data Mining, pp. 133–142 (2002)
16. Li, Q., et al.: A survey on text classification: from traditional to deep learning. ACM Trans. Intell. Syst. Technol. **13**(2), 1–41 (2022)
17. Liu, B., Li, X., Lee, W.S., Yu, P.S.: Text classification by labeling words. In: AAAI, vol. 4, pp. 425–430 (2004)
18. Liu, S., Lee, I.: Email sentiment analysis through k-means labeling and support vector machine classification. Cybern. Syst. **49**(3), 181–199 (2018)
19. Read, J.: Using emoticons to reduce dependency in machine learning techniques for sentiment classification. In: Proceedings of the ACL Student Research Workshop, pp. 43–48 (2005)
20. Reddy, Y., Viswanath, P., Reddy, B.E.: Semi-supervised learning: a brief review. Int. J. Eng. Technol. **7**(1.8), 81 (2018)
21. Rosso, P., Errecalde, M., Pinto, D.: Analysis of short texts on the web: introduction to special issue. Lang. Resour. Eval. **47**(1), 123–126 (2013)
22. Salton, G., Wong, A., Yang, C.S.: A vector space model for automatic indexing. Commun. ACM **18**(11), 613–620 (1975)

23. Silva, N.F.F.D., Coletta, L.F., Hruschka, E.R.: A survey and comparative study of tweet sentiment analysis via semi-supervised learning. ACM Comput. Surv. **49**(1), 1–26 (2016)
24. Skiena, S.S.: The Data Science Design Manual. Springer, Cham (2017). https://doi.org/10.1007/978-3-319-55444-0
25. Sneiders, E., Sjöbergh, J., Alfalahi, A.: Automated email answering by text-pattern matching: performance and error analysis. Expert. Syst. **35**(1), e12251 (2018)
26. Statista: Most popular global mobile messenger apps as of July 2019, based on number of monthly active users (in millions) (2019). http://www.statista.com/
27. Tang, G., Pei, J., Luk, W.-S.: Email mining: tasks, common techniques, and tools. Knowl. Inf. Syst. **41**(1), 1–31 (2013). https://doi.org/10.1007/s10115-013-0658-2
28. Usai, A., Pironti, M., Mital, M., Mejri, C.A.: Knowledge discovery out of text data: a systematic review via text mining. J. Knowl. Manag. (2018)
29. van Engelen, J.E., Hoos, H.H.: A survey on semi-supervised learning. Mach. Learn. **109**(2), 373–440 (2019). https://doi.org/10.1007/s10994-019-05855-6
30. Vaswani, A., et al.: Attention is all you need. arXiv preprint arXiv:1706.03762 (2017)
31. Zhou, Z.H., Zhan, D.C., Yang, Q.: Semi-supervised learning with very few labeled training examples. In: AAAI, vol. 675680 (2007)

Applying Game-Learning Environments to Power Capping Scenarios via Reinforcement Learning

Pablo Hernández, Luis Costero$^{(\boxtimes)}$, Katzalin Olcoz, and Francisco D. Igual

Departamento de Arquitectura de Computadores y Automática,
Universidad Complutense de Madrid, Madrid, Spain
{pherna06,lcostero,katzalin,figual}@ucm.es

Abstract. Research in deep learning for video game playing has received much attention and provided very relevant results in the last years. Frameworks and libraries have been developed to ease game playing research leveraging Reinforcement Learning techniques. In this paper, we propose to use two of them (RLLIB and GYM) in a very different scenario, such as learning to apply resource management policies in a multi-core server, specifically, we leverage the facilities of both frameworks coupled to derive policies for power-capping. Using RLLIB and GYM enables implementing different resource management policies in a simple and fast way and, as they are based on neural networks, guarantees the efficiency in the solution, and the use of hardware accelerators for both training and inference. The results demonstrate that game-learning environments provide an effective support to cast a completely different scenario, and open new research avenues in the field of resource management using reinforcement learning techniques with minimal development effort.

Keywords: Reinforcement Learning · RLLIB · GYM · Resource management · Power capping · DVFS

1 Introduction

Artificial Intelligence (AI) has been widely used in video games for quite a long time, both for improving the user experience playing the game, and also developing automatic systems that learn how to win them [18]. In October 2015, AlphaGo, an algorithm based on Deep Reinforcement Learning (RL), beat one of the best human players, reaching a milestone in AI research for video game playing [19]. Nowadays, deep learning for video game playing is an active area of research [13]. The goal of these systems is to automatically learn policies that win the game, with *agents* interacting with an *environment* and the achieved score as a *reward* to be maximized.

In response to the increasing interest in learning environments for games, different platforms and software ecosystems have emerged to improve both the quality and the efficiency of the learning process. Among them, the tuple RLLIB–GYM[1] is one of the most successful efforts. GYM provides an abstraction for the construction of *environments* that can be interacted externally by means of the application of actions, and sensed afterwards. This abstraction facilitates the development process, and the definition of new environments with complex behaviors, maintaining the external interface. RLLIB is a complete distributed infrastructure that provides a plethora of RL agent development primitives that, together with a GYM environment, can yield policies in an easy way, leveraging high performance computing strategies.

Environments provide an abstraction to build ad-hoc *black boxes* that mimic the behaviour of virtually any stateful scenario, with the possibility of receiving actions, modifying (and observing) the internal state of the environment and receiving back a proper reward depending on the target optimization objective. The behaviour of an environment can be easily personalized, maintaining a common external interface for an easy interaction and deployment. In this paper, we leverage this abstraction to propose the application of the aforementioned game-specific frameworks, to a dramatically different scenario: *power capping* on modern multi-core servers. *Power capping* [25] is a strategy typically applied in different datacenter-level scenarios to limit instantaneous power consumption at different levels (chip, server, facility, etc.), in order to fulfill user-specific limits, or system-wide power restrictions.

Modern multi-core servers exhibit a number of knobs that can directly impact power consumption; one of the most effective is DVFS (*Dynamic Voltage-Frequency Scaling*) that, assisted with the appropriate operating system support, can adapt the effective operating frequency at different granularities. Additionally, modern processors are armed with different mechanisms to measure the instantaneous power consumption at different levels (usually per core, socket and complete system). All in all, a computing server equipped with DVFS and capabilities to measure power consumption can be considered as an ideal scenario for a complete interaction with a RL agent, as it:

- Provides a stable *observation space*, in terms of sensed power consumption.
- Features a set of *actions* with impact on the observed power consumption.
- In a *power capping* scenario, allows the design and implementation of a convenient *reward* strategy that penalizes power states above the specified power cap, and positively rewards power states below the power cap.

We explore the feasibility of extending state-of-the-art RL libraries widely used in the video game arena, to a power capping scenario. Specifically, we will show how a power capping scenario can be easily modelled as a RL problem, and how little effort is required to implement it in terms of existing software infrastructure. A discussion of how state and action definition impacts on the outcome policy will also be presented. Additionally, we will show how the described approach can deal with different workloads (in terms of different power demands) and with different power capping limits.

---

[1] https://docs.ray.io/en/latest/rllib.html – https://gym.openai.com/.

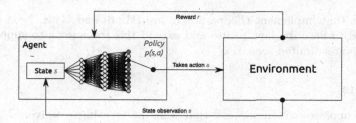

Fig. 1. General overview of a Reinforcement Learning process.

The rest of this paper is organized as follows: Sect. 2 describes how a RL algorithm works in general, and how it is implemented in Ray and RLLIB in particular. Section 3 provides a detailed motivation of our effort towards leveraging existing RL libraries for Resource Management, and compares our approach with the state-of-the-art. Section 4 shows how a power capping scenario can be expressed in terms of the previous libraries. We report experimental results in Sect. 5. Related work is shown in Sect. 6 and concluding remarks in Sect. 7.

2   The RLLIB and GYM Frameworks

Reinforcement Learning [22] is one of the three basic pillars of Machine Learning, together with *Supervised* and *Unsupervised learning*. It is oriented towards training a system by interacting with its environment, to automatically determine its ideal behaviour in a specific context, so that its profit is maximized. This general goal is usually tackled by means of agent-environment paradigms, in which one (or multiple) agent decides the actions that the environment needs to perform, based on its state or observation. The agent receives a numeric value (*reward*), calculated as a function of the previous environment state, and the current state after applying an action. This way, the agent can *learn* which actions must be taken by the environment to maximize the cumulative reward. Different RL algorithms implement different methods to obtain these policies (e.g., table-based solutions as Q-Learning, or Neural Network based solutions as DQN [16]). The benefit of using Neural Netwoks as a function approximator is three-fold: *(i)* they scale in performance for large action-state spaces; *(ii)* they can leverage software frameworks (e.g. Tensorflow) for efficient implementations; and *(iii)* domain-specific hardware can be used to accelerate their execution. Figure 1 depicts this process.

RL has been successfully applied to game-learning systems in order to infer, learn and apply game rules by means of observation and interaction with existing game engines with minimum level of environmental knowledge. A representative example is DQN, a complex Deep Reinforcement Learning architecture that is able to learn policies directly from high-dimensional sensory inputs; specifically, DQN receives only the pixels and the game score as inputs, and is able to surpass a human games tester on a wide range of games. Two of the most popular frameworks that implement this paradigm are RLLIB and GYM. Next sections are devoted to describe how to use and extend this framework to support and manage a power-limited scenario.

2.1   RLLIB

Ray is an open-source framework that aims at creating a universal API for *distributed applications*. Within the framework, the Python library RLLIB is focused on supporting Reinforcement Learning applications at all necessary levels. RAY/RLLIB offer facilities to parallelize code across shared- or distributed-memory architectures, optionally equipped with accelerators (GPUs). Internally, RLLIB uses TENSORFLOW to model the complete structure of a RL problem and to integrate models (neural networks) that mimic the approximation functions necessary on RL problems.

2.2   GYM

GYM is an open-source library designed to develop and compare RL algorithms. GYM includes a rich collection of *environments* that allow an interaction with agents trained via reinforcement learning. The interaction with these environments mimics the general idea of reinforcement learning: the agent can apply a number of actions on an environment (the exact set of actions is defined in the GYM environment) and, as a result, the GYM environment returns a tuple of values, including the obtained *reward* and the new *observation*. GYM is mainly focused on game learning, but offers mechanisms to define new environments based on an API that allows a straightforward and portable interaction with the environment from an external agent. This API orbits around two main routines:

- reset(): that obtains an initial *state observation* from the environment.
- step(action): invoked by an agent, and receiving an action to apply (an integer within a range of pre-determined values).

The step() routine returns information of the effect of the action on the environment, including:

- observation: object representing a new observation after the application of an action. Its type and range of values depend on the specific environment.
- reward: reward obtained after the application of a new action on the environment in a given state. It is represented as a floating point number and its range is also defined by the specific environment.
- done: optional value that indicates the end of the environment lifetime.
- info: dictionary with additional debugging information, including information regarding the evolution of the learning process.

Each environment features an *action space* ($\mathcal{A}$) and an *observation space* ($\mathcal{S}$), that define the values that can be taken as actions (hence, the shape of the output tensor of the underlying neural network) and the values that can be obtained as an observation (hence, the shape of the input tensor). Additionally, a reward function ($\mathcal{R}$) that gives a score to each action applied by the agent is used to train the system and obtain the desired policy ($\mathcal{R} : \mathcal{S} \times \mathcal{S} \times \mathcal{A} \to \mathbb{R}$).

Obtaining a suitable RL policy is just the task of training the underlying neural network. This task is transparently carried out by the RLLIB framework by means of interacting with the GYM environment.

3   RL for Resource Management

Computer architectures have evolved drastically in the last decades, seeking an optimal combination of performance and energy efficiency in response to the growing demands of modern software. The strategies followed in early-2000s, mainly dictated by a constant increase of the frequency, cannot be further pursued due to the lack of technological support, keeping core frequencies around 2–4 GHz to keep heat and power under control [1], leading to a shift towards multi-core architectures, and therefore alleviating the task of computer architects to improve energy efficiency. Together with the increase in the number of compute units, the addition of different technologies that allow processors to adapt dynamically to the changes in the environment and running applications has accompanied the processor evolution. DVFS [3], Power Capping [7] or Cache Partitioning [8] are only three examples of hardware-assisted support to increase performance and/or energy efficiency. In addition, this type of systems usually expose a number of mechanisms to measure (or estimate) different metrics with different granularity (e.g., modern processors offer mechanisms to measure energy at a core, socket, and system level).

This evolution has provoked a change in how resources are managed. In the past, Resource Managers had to deal with simple scenarios with a limited number of parameters to configure and metrics to monitor. Nowadays, architectures offer a plethora of different metrics to observe, and parameters to tune (possibly simultaneously), leading to more complex scenarios. Specifically, modern resource managers need to deal with:

1. *Malleability at system-level:* Modern platforms support a plethora of different mechanisms to adapt themselves to the running applications and environments. Examples are DVFS capabilities, support for core disabling/enabling, or cache partitioning. In addition, one metric can be affected by multiple parameters, and one parameter can have effects on multiple metrics at the same time, making the process of designing the policy an arduous task.
2. *Malleability at application-level:* Modern applications expose a number of parameters that can be configured statically and dynamically, and affect directly to different application- and system-metrics (e.g., changes on the number of threads used during the computations). These parameters should be considered together with system-parameters to obtain the best results.
3. *Multiple optimization goals:* As platforms and applications have evolved, their requirements have evolved too. Modern resource managers should seek to

fulfill multiple optimization goals at the same time (e.g., energy efficiency, performance, Quality of Experience (QoE), etc.). However, designing a multi-objective system is not a trivial task.

4. *Additional restrictions:* Apart from the optimization goals defined by the system designer, applications and platforms can present additional restrictions that the resource manager has to fulfill (e.g., power capping limits, minimum Quality of Service (QoS) requirements, etc.).

In this scenario, a main question arises: *how can we obtain a multi-objective resource management policy able to modify multiple parameters concurrently at the same time it deals with the previous problems?*

Traditionally, complex heuristics have been used as the *de-facto* solution to manage shared resources in computing platforms [10,20]. On one hand, heuristics are simple solutions to these problems, yielding easy-to-understand policies. On the other hand, a deep knowledge of the problem is required to design effective heuristics. In addition, the obtained policies are usually valid only for a specific set of fixed conditions, and dependent on the problem input.

With the increasing interest on Machine Learning, RL has been proved as a valid alternative to tackle these scenarios [5,12], as it presents several advantages over the traditional approaches. Among others, a less deep knowledge of the problem is required to formulate the solution, as well as the ability to obtain input-independent policies. As drawbacks, ML-based approaches can lead to long training periods, as well as to solutions that, being valid, are difficult to understand by a human compared with heuristics. However, although the use of RL is widely extended in other fields (as videogames), the application of these techniques to resource management is far from being trivial, and typically requires ad-hoc implementations [5,12].

4   Casting a Power Capping Scenario with GYM

Our contribution lies on the design of GYM environments that tackle the afore-mentioned *power capping* scenario. The proposed environments implement *(i)* an observation space that can be filled by ad-hoc power measurement mechanisms (in our case, Intel RAPL); *(ii)* an action space, in which actions can range from selecting specific frequencies between those offered by the processor, to increase/decrease on an individual step basis; and *(iii)* a specific *reward* strategy, that implements techniques to fulfill a specific goal (e.g. maximizing performance under a power cap).

All this logic is encapsulated within a GYM environment that keeps the same interface as that previously described. Armed with this type of environments, we integrate them in the RLLIB environment and apply training procedures to determine the ability of the system to extract efficient policies that, deployed on a real multi-core server, can keep the power consumption under an established cap for different workloads. Figure 2 shows the original game-learning environment and the modifications that are needed in order to obtain a power capping policy. Only two python modules are needed: pyRAPL, that obtains energy measurements

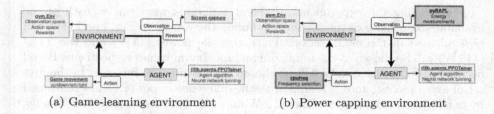

(a) Game-learning environment   (b) Power capping environment

Fig. 2. RLLIB-based implementation applied to video games (left) and power capping (right). Note that minimum changes are needed (marked in red). (Color figure online)

used as observations, and `cpufreq`, that applies the changes in frequency that correspond to the different actions chosen. The remainder of this section shows how to create a new environment, defining the set of actions, states and rewards.

4.1 Defining States

The observation space is formed by the different values of power consumed by the system. Even if this value is a real number, we will use a discrete number of states, each one comprising all the power consumption values in a given range. However, there is not any golden rule about how states, actions and rewards have to be defined, and expert knowledge of the problem is required. Their definition, and specially the number of actions and states will ultimately determine the quality of the learned policy as well as the training time required to obtain a functional policy [4]. On one hand, if each state covers a wide range of power values, the learning time will decrease as the number of states to explore will be lower. However, the quality of the obtained policy may be negatively affected as the system will not be able to apply different actions to different values in the same interval. On the other, increasing the number of states (i.e., decreasing the power interval covered by each state) will improve the quality of the policy as the agent will be able to apply actions in a finer granularity, at the expenses of longer learning times, since the agent will need to explore more states.

So, different alternatives for the definition of states and actions will be explored in this work. In our first formulation of the problem, there will be one state for all the power values lower than a certain power value, another for all the power values greater than another certain value, and the interval between those two values will be divided in equally sized states of a specific size.

In order to choose these three values (minimum power value, maximum power value, and interval size), some profiling is required, so that the minimum and maximum power consumption values can be identified. After that, the minimum power value will be the consumption when the system is in idle, and the maximum power value will correspond with the TDP of the machine (or maximum power measured). Additionally, the size of the interval will be certain value that guarantees that the power measurements obtained at different frequencies during the profiling phase are not classified into the same state.

For running the experiments, different programs were run at each of the available frequencies of the system, obtaining the results in Fig. 3 and that will be explained in the next section. Thus, the idle power (15 W) and the TDP (115 W) will be chosen as the minimum and maximum values respectively. Based on the results, a size of 3 W will be chosen for creating the intervals in the first set of experiments, since it is similar to the difference in power values consumed by two adjacent frequencies. Sizes of 2 W and 4 W will be also explored. Finally, other configuration with non-uniform distribution of states will be tried.

4.2 Defining Actions and Rewards

Similar to the state definition, the number of actions will ultimately determine the quality of the obtained policy, as well as the learning time (greater number of actions usually means greater quality at expenses of longer training periods). In our first environment, we consider the actions limited to increase one step the current frequency, and to decrease one step the frequency. If the action is not available (i.e., maximum/minimum frequency is already set and the agent is trying to increase/decrease the frequency), no action is applied. Other definitions are possible, like considering all the available frequencies as possible actions for the agent. Nevertheless, a different set of actions will be considered later, that includes the posibility of maintaining the frequency at the same level.

The reward function is defined based on how good or bad is the action taken compared with the previous step. More specifically, the reward given at step $t+1$ (R_{t+1}) is defined as follows:

$$R_{t+1}(s_t, s_{t+1}) = \begin{cases} -1 & \text{if} \quad |s_{t+1} - s_{goal}| > |s_t - s_{goal}| \\ +1 & \text{if} \quad |s_{t+1} - s_{goal}| < |s_t - s_{goal}| \\ +2 & \text{if} \quad s_{t+1} - s_{goal} = 0 \end{cases} \qquad (1)$$

where s_{t+1} and s_t are the states the system is in the current and previous steps respectively, and s_{goal} is the state containing the established power cap.

This reward definition guarantees that the system will move closer to the desired power consumption at each step. Indeed, the reward will penalize the agent if the new power observation is farther from the cap than the previously observed power (reward of -1), will give a reward of $+1$ if the new power observation is closer than the previous one, and will grant a maximum reward of $+2$ if the power observation is in the same interval as the established cap.

5 Experimental Results

All experiments were implemented on a real server comprising two Intel Xeon CPUs E5-2670 with a total of 16 physical cores and 64 GB of DRAM. Thermal Design Power (TDP) is 115 W for each processor. Available frequencies range from 1200 MHz to 2600 MHz, selectable with a 100 MHz granularity. The following libraries (and versions) were used in the experiments: Python (3.8.5),

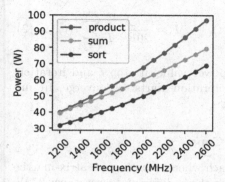 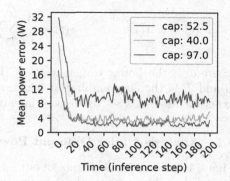

Fig. 3. Power consumption profile for the different workloads.

Fig. 4. Mean power error for different power cap limits.

`cpufreq` (0.3.3), `pyRAPL` (0.2.3.1), `GYM` (0.17.3), `Ray` (1.0.1), and `NumPy` (1.18.5). Multiple power capping values were considered to prove the validity of our approach.

All environments have been tested via RLLIB with different background workloads: matrix-matrix multiplication (called `product` in the following), vector sort (`sort`) and matrix-matrix addition (`sum`), all using floating point elements. Each experiment was initialized with a different frequency, covering all the possible values. This selection covers a number of different functional units usage, and hence power consumption requirements. Each experiment was repeated 15 times with different initial frequency values. Figure 3 shows the different power values measured for the previous workloads at different frequencies. Matrix-based operations (`product` and `sum`) were configured to use $1,000 \times 1,000$ elements, while a vector of $1,000,000$ elements was used for the sorting operation. Observe how these workloads cover all the possible range of power values for the different frequency values tested, and how the benchmarks exhibit a different behaviour as the frequency increases, covering different situations present on real-life scenarios.

To avoid noisy measurements, the Reinforcement Learning process was run in a different socket than the one workloads are run and frequency is change. Additionally, library was configures to train only one agent simultaneously, avoiding possible interference between agents. Power measurements correspond to average power consumption measured during 150 ms. In addition, the following 100 ms after a frequency change were not measured to not introduce noise in the system. For training the system, a total of 5 epochs were run, with 4000 steps in each epoch, each of 250 ms. These values guarantee that the Reinforcement learning process does not influence on the learning process. The `product` workload was used on this phase. For testing each learned policy, 15 iterations of 200 steps each were run. For each iteration, the environment was initialized with a different frequency to test all the scenarios. Numerical results of each tested policy are presented in terms of mean error ($\epsilon(t)$) and mean accumulated error (E), defined as follows:

$$\epsilon^j(t) = |x^j(t) - \overline{x}|, \qquad \epsilon(t) = \frac{1}{15} \sum_{j=1}^{15} \epsilon^j(t), \qquad E = \frac{1}{201 - T} \sum_{t=T}^{200} \epsilon(t) \qquad (2)$$

where $\overline{x}$ is the power target, $x^j(t)$ is the power value at step t and iteration j, and T is the step number at which the iteration starts to converge. In our experiments T was set to 75 experimentally.

5.1   Analysis Under Different Power Caps

Figure 4 shows a detailed trace of our approach when executing a matrix-matrix **product** workload in the background under three different power caps: 97 W ($\approx$84% TDP), 52.5 W ($\approx$46% TDP) and 40 W ($\approx$35% TDP). This three values mimic possible values present in real-life scenarios. The simple definition of states (fixed size of 3 W) and actions (increase/decrease frequency) was used.

As observed, our approach exhibits a similar behaviour for all the tested power caps: a first phase with constant decreasing error values, and a second phase where the system has converged and the error keeps relatively constant ($t \geq 75$). This is the result of how the experiments were carried out. Indeed, as the initial frequencies of the 15 testing iterations cover the whole frequency spectrum, the agent needs to modify the frequency several times until an ideal frequency producing power values near the required value is reached. However, when comparing the three approaches, the error obtained when the power cap is close to the limit is significantly higher than for the other values. This behaviour is a direct consequence of the available actions of the agent. For a high power cap, the optimal policy should maintain the frequency to the maximum most of the time. However, our agent definition does not consider this option, being constantly oscillating between the two highest frequencies. We show how this behaviour can be improved in the next subsection. Nevertheless, our approach is able to maintain the system with a power consumption close to the power cap, with an average accumulated error (E) of 3.68 W, 2.42 W and 9.49 W for 40 W, 52.5 W and 97 W power cap values respectively.

Figure 5 offers an intuitive vision of the convergence of the training algorithm, when establishing a power cap of 52.5 W. Observe how, as the training process proceeds, the agent takes less random decisions (in terms of frequency selection), and the observed power converges to the target cap.

5.2   Impact of the State and Action Definitions

Figure 6 shows the mean power error (ϵ) for three different state definitions, each with a different power interval size (2 W, 3 W and 4 W), configured in the same environment described before with a target power cap of 52.5 W. The mean accumulated error (E) is 2.54 W, 2.42 W and 2.71 W respectively. Observe how, for this specific scenario, the policy obtained in each case produces similar results. This is due to the reduced number of actions the agent has to consider at each state. Indeed, the agent will potentially take the same action for all the

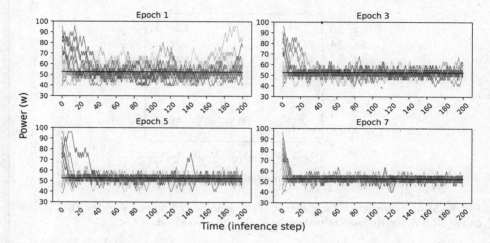

Fig. 5. Power consumption for different training epochs, using a matrix-matrix `product` workload. The black line represents the target power cap. Each other color represent a different iteration with a different initial frequency.

power values in the same interval, producing the same results independently on how big or small is each one. This behaviour will be different only in those states close to the power cap imposed. However, the number of these states is negligible in comparison with the amount of states far from this value.

To test how different state/action definitions impact our scenario, two additional environments (apart from the one defined) were defined:

- Env2: same strategy as Env1, but an additional action to maintain the frequency at the same level was added. Thanks to this modification, the agent can potentially learn to maintain the frequency when the power measurements are close to the power cap, decreasing the error.
- Env3: An extension of Env2, but performing a non-uniform distribution of the observation space. This distribution is based on the power profiling from a specific workload (matrix-matrix `product`). For each power value measured, a new state was created containing this value but not any other value measured. Considered actions are the same as in the previous environment.

Table 1 summarizes the configuration of the aforementioned environments, and the parameters of the underlying neural network in terms of number of inputs, neurons per layer, number of outputs and trainable parameters.

Figure 7 and Table 2 report the mean power error (ϵ) and mean accumulated error (E) respectively for the three different power caps tested. Overall, observe that Env2 and Env3 obtain low and similar error values (ϵ and E), while the policy associated to Env1 produces worse results. This is a direct consequence of adding to the agent the option to maintain the frequency, that improves drastically the results for all the tested power caps, with improvements of $2\times$, $11\times$ and $10\times$ for 52.5 W, 40 W and 97 W respectively in the mean accumulated error (E) when

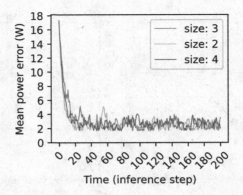

Fig. 6. Mean power error for different state definitions (interval sizes) with a power cap of 52.5 W for the matrix-matrix multiplication workload.

Table 1. Overview of the different tested environments.

	State definition	Actions	Neural network				
			Inputs	L1	L2	Outputs	Trainable parameters
Env1	Uniform (3 W)	↑/↓ freq.	37	256	256	2	151,811
Env2	Uniform (3 W)	↑/↓/↔ freq.	37	256	256	3	152,068
Env3	Non-uniform	↑/↓/↔ freq.	16	256	256	3	141,316

compared with Env2, and 2×, 9×, and 8× when compared against Env3. Lastly, observe that there is not too much difference between environments Env2 and Env3. However, using custom intervals for the state definition (Env3) allow us to reduce the number of states drastically from 36 in Env2 to 15 in Env3, and therefore, reduce the learning time (or equivalently, obtain a policy with greater quality for the same learning time) at the cost of loosing generality.

5.3   Behaviour Under Different Workloads

To show the effectiveness of our approach under different workloads, the environment Env2 was trained running matrix-matrix multiplications (product) in the background and tested against the other two operations described above (i.e., matrix-matrix addition -sum- and vector sorting -sort-). Figure 8a shows the mean power error (ϵ) produced for the different workloads with a power cap of 52.5 W. As observed, for both matrix-matrix multiplications and matrix-matrix addition, the results are similar, producing an average error of 1 W respect to the power cap. However, a greater error is obtained when the sort workload is run in the background. This error is the consequence of the different power consumption each workload has (see Fig. 3). Indeed, the sort operation presents power values that are not produced by any of the other benchmarks at any frequency.

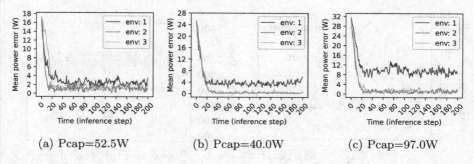

(a) Pcap=52.5W   (b) Pcap=40.0W   (c) Pcap=97.0W

Fig. 7. Mean power error for different power cap limits and actions when running the matrix-matrix multiplication workload in background.

Table 2. Mean accumulated error (E) under different power caps.

	Env1			Env2			Env3		
Pcap	52.5 W	40.0 W	97.0 W	52.5 W	40.0 W	97.0 W	52.5 W	40.0 W	97.0 W
	2.42 W	3.68 W	9.49 W	1.17 W	0.34 W	0.98 W	1.25 W	0.39 W	1.25 W

As a consequence, because the system was trained using the `product` operation as workload, the agent still has some states not explored when running with the `sort` operation in background, leading the agent to take actions randomly. This behaviour can be seen more clearly in Fig. 8b, that shows the frequency taken by the agent at each iteration. As observed, although most of the actions are centered around 2200 MHz, there are noisy actions far from this value. This behaviour ultimately produces the high error values described before.

These results reveal the importance of the input used for training, and how if a workload able to produce all the different power values (or a mixed of multiple workloads) is used, the obtained policy will yield better results.

6   Related Work

Our work brings contributions in two different areas: *(i)* resource management via RL, and *(ii)* power capping management on modern multi-core systems.

Traditionally, resource management has been tackled by the creation of heuristics and model-based solutions [2,9]. However, these techniques tend to create input-specific solutions, being difficult to extrapolate them to a more general scenario. On the contrary, Machine Learning solutions present a novel approach to obtain generic solutions. Multiple authors have proposed different approaches targeting different objectives in the past (performance, energy efficiency, power consumption, etc.). For example, a solution using RL to model a system is proposed in [11]. However, this approach lacks of generality to be

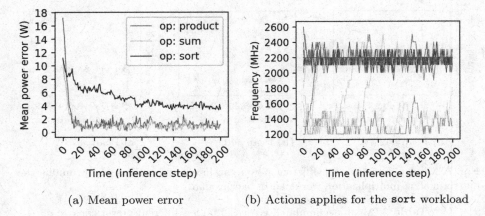

(a) Mean power error   (b) Actions applies for the `sort` workload

Fig. 8. Behaviour of the system under different workloads and a power cap of 52.5 W. On the left, mean power error. On the right, actions taken by the agent (i.e., frequency set) for the `sort` workload at epoch 5.

applied to other scenarios described in the paper. Contrary to the previous approaches, [6] and [15] propose rule-based systems to tune multiple application- and system-metrics. However, the rules described in these works have to be made specifically to the system, lacking of enough generality.

Targeting power-capping, several approaches have been proposed to keep processors under strict power limits like [7,14]. Additionally to these restrictions, several proposed systems have incorporated performance as an additional metric to tune, like [17,23], which base their decisions in heuristics, and [21,24] that present model-based solutions. Contrary to our proposal, all the previous approaches require a deep knowledge of the system, and feature ad-hoc implementations, difficult to extend to any other system and yielding time-consuming and error-prone development methodologies.

7   Conclusions

In this paper, we have given clues and evidences towards the integration of power capping mechanisms within frameworks (RLlib and *Gym*) that are conceived and designed for other type of domains. By means of abstracting observations, actions and rewards, we have shown how existing Reinforcement Learning frameworks can obtain efficient policies to automatically apply power capping techniques by software. This idea opens a plethora of research lines, including the acceleration of the training processes via multiple hardware accelerators, provided the underlying infrastructure supports this kind of functionality. The integration of Domain-Specific Accelerators (e.g. TPUs) for inference is one of the most promising research lines in our roadmap, leveraging the neural-network-based approach followed in RLLIB.

We have experimentally proven how our proposal is able to control the power consumption of a system running different workloads, each with a different power-consumption profile. All the experiments were run considering different power cap values, making them generic enough to be applicable to other scenarios. Additionally, we have shown how the state and action definitions influence in the quality of the policy obtained. In particular, adding an action to the original environment has proved to decrease the obtained error by $2\times$, $11\times$ and $10\times$ for executions with a power cap of 52.5 W, 40 W and 97 W respectively.

Acknowledgements. This work was supported by the EU (FEDER) and Spanish MINECO (RTI2018-093684-B-I00), and Comunidad de Madrid under the Multiannual Agreement with Complutense University in the line Program to Stimulate Research for Young Doctors in the context of the V PRICIT under projects PR65/19-22445 and CM S2018/TCS-4423.

References

1. Barroso, L.A.: The price of performance: an economic case for chip multiprocessing. Queue **3**(7), 48–53 (2005)
2. Bartolini, A., Cacciari, M., Tilli, A., Benini, L.: Thermal and energy management of high-performance multicores: distributed and self-calibrating model-predictive controller. IEEE Trans. Parallel Distrib. Syst. **24**(1), 170–183 (2013)
3. Calore, E., Gabbana, A., Schifano, S.F., Tripiccione, R.: Evaluation of DVFS techniques on modern HPC processors and accelerators for energy-aware applications. Concurr. Comput. Pract. Exp. **29**(12), e4143 (2017)
4. Costero, L., Igual, F.D., Olcoz, K., Tirado, F.: Leveraging knowledge-as-a-service (KaaS) for QoS-aware resource management in multi-user video transcoding. J. Supercomput. **76**(12), 9388–9403 (2020). https://doi.org/10.1007/s11227-019-03117-9
5. Costero, L., Iranfar, A., Zapater, M., Igual, F.D., Olcoz, K., Atienza, D.: Resource management for power-constrained HEVC transcoding using reinforcement learning. IEEE Trans. Parallel Distrib. Syst. **31**(12), 2834–2850 (2020)
6. Donyanavard, B., et al.: SOSA: self-optimizing learning with self-adaptive control for hierarchical system-on-chip management. In: Proceedings of the 52nd Annual IEEE/ACM International Symposium on Microarchitecture (2019)
7. Felter, W., Rajamani, K., Keller, T., Rusu, C.: A performance-conserving approach for reducing peak power consumption in server systems. In: Proceedings of the 19th Annual International Conference on Supercomputing (2005)
8. Garcia-Garcia, A., Saez, J.C., Risco-Martin, J.L., Prieto-Matias, M.: PBBCache: an open-source parallel simulator for rapid prototyping and evaluation of cache-partitioning and cache-clustering policies. J. Comput. Sci. **42**, 101102 (2020)
9. Gupta, U., et al.: Dynamic power budgeting for mobile systems running graphics workloads. IEEE TMSCS **4**(1), 30–40 (2018)
10. Hanumaiah, V., Desai, D., Gaudette, B., Wu, C.J., Vrudhula, S.: STEAM: a smart temperature and energy aware multicore controller. ACM Trans. Embed. Comput. Syst. **13**(5s), 1–25 (2014)
11. Ho, H.N., Lee, E.: Model-based reinforcement learning approach for planning in self-adaptive software system. In: Proceedings of the 9th International Conference on Ubiquitous Information Management and Communication (2015)

12. Iranfar, A., Zapater, M., Atienza, D.: Machine learning-based quality-aware power and thermal management of multistream HEVC encoding on multicore servers. IEEE Trans. Parallel Distrib. Syst. **29**(10), 2268–2281 (2018)

13. Justesen, N., Bontrager, P., Togelius, J., Risi, S.: Deep learning for video game playing. IEEE Trans. Games **12**(1), 1–20 (2020)

14. Lefurgy, C., Wang, X., Ware, M.: Power capping: a prelude to power shifting. Clust. Comput. **11**(2), 183–195 (2008). https://doi.org/10.1007/s10586-007-0045-4

15. Maurer, F., Donyanavard, B., Rahmani, A.M., Dutt, N., Herkersdorf, A.: Emergent control of MPSoC operation by a hierarchical supervisor/reinforcement learning approach. In: Design, Automation and Test in Europe Conference and Exhibition (2020)

16. Mnih, V., et al.: Human-level control through deep reinforcement learning. Nature **518**(7540), 529–533 (2015)

17. Petrica, P., Izraelevitz, A.M., Albonesi, D.H., Shoemaker, C.A.: Flicker: a dynamically adaptive architecture for power limited multicore systems. In: Proceedings of the 40th Annual International Symposium on Computer Architecture (2013)

18. Shao, K., Tang, Z., Zhu, Y., Li, N., Zhao, D.: A survey of deep reinforcement learning in video games (2019)

19. Silver, D., et al.: Mastering the game of go without human knowledge. Nature **550**, 354–359 (2017)

20. Singh, A.K., Prakash, A., Basireddy, K.R., Merrett, G.V., Al-Hashimi, B.M.: Energy-efficient run-time mapping and thread partitioning of concurrent OpenCL applications on CPU-GPU MPSoCs. ACM Trans. Embed. Comput. Syst. **16**(5s), 1–22 (2017)

21. Singla, G., Kaur, G., Unver, A.K., Ogras, U.Y.: Predictive dynamic thermal and power management for heterogeneous mobile platforms. In: Design, Automation and Test in Europe Conference and Exhibition (2015)

22. Sutton, R.S., Barto, A.G.: Reinforcement Learning: An introduction, vol. 1. MIT Press, Cambridge (1998)

23. Teodorescu, R., Torrellas, J.: Variation-aware application scheduling and power management for chip multiprocessors. ACM SIGARCH Comput. Archit. News **36**(3), 363–374 (2008)

24. Yan, K., Zhang, X., Tan, J., Xin, F.: Redefining QoS and customizing the power management policy to satisfy individual mobile users. In: 49th Annual IEEE/ACM International Symposium on Microarchitecture (MICRO) (2016)

25. Zhang, H., Hoffmann, H.: Maximizing performance under a power cap: a comparison of hardware, software, and hybrid techniques. ACM SIGPLAN Not. **51**(4), 545–559 (2016)

Solving an Instance of a Routing Problem Through Reinforcement Learning and High Performance Computing

Esteban Schab[1,3]([✉]) [iD], Carlos Casanova[1,3] [iD], and Fabiana Piccoli[2,3] [iD]

[1] Facultad Regional Concepción del Uruguay, Universidad Tecnológica Nacional, Buenos Aires, Argentina
{schabe,casanovac}@frcu.utn.edu.ar
[2] Universidad Nacional de San Luis, Ejército de los Andes 950, San Luis, Argentina
mpiccoli@unsl.edu.ar
[3] Universidad Autónoma de Entre Ríos, 25 de Mayo 385, Concepción del Uruguay, Entre Ríos, Argentina

Abstract. Today, data management is important, mainly in organizations where the real-time processing of a large number of events is important to decision-making systems. Analyzing large amounts of data through analytics allows discovering hidden knowledge and make decisions in consequence. In this work, we propose to solve a decision-making problem in real-time using prescriptive analytics model, reinforcement learning agents and parallel computing techniques in GPU. Particularly, we consider the vehicle routing problem (VRP) with real-time information provision and re-routing. The experimental results confirm that the adequate combination of these techniques is a promising option for solving this kind of problem.

Keywords: Computational intelligence · Agents · Reinforcement learning · High performance computing · GPGPU · TensorFlow

1 Introduction

Continuous and adaptive improvement of business processes is a key issue for organizations when they intend to be competitive. In this sense, the digitalization of processes, as well as the increase in monitoring technologies, have produced a large amount of data (Massive Data or Big Data). This implies a great potential for the improvement of processes driven by analytics [7, 26, 35].

Analytics seek to transform data into decision-making knowledge [12]. There are four analytics types that are distinguishable according to their level of automation of their process [22]. In order, we find:

- Descriptive analytics: It attempts to answer what has happened or what is happening.
- Diagnostic analytics: It points to why has it happened or why is it happening.

E. Rucci et al. (Eds.): JCC-BD&ET 2022, CCIS 1634, pp. 107–121, 2022.
https://doi.org/10.1007/978-3-031-14599-5_8

- Predictive analytics: It applies knowledge to predict new data about the present or the future (forecasts). It seeks to answer what will happen.
- Prescriptive analytics: It pretends to answer what should be done and how it could be done. It calculates actions to be executed at the moment (operational decisions) or in the future (tactical decisions: short and medium term, or strategic: long term).

The first three approaches do not suggest concrete actions, but they depend on the subjective judgment and analytical skills of the user, who must deduce and evaluate the possible improvement actions. Descriptive and Diagnostic analytics base their work on historical data.

Nowadays, most process analytics do not take full advantage of the knowledge hidden in the large volumes of data, they have the following limitations:

1. Lack of use of prescriptive techniques to transform the analysis results into concrete improvement actions. This step is left to the user's subjective criterion.
2. Data-intensive use of systems in production. This implies a performance loss of the software tools involved in processes.
3. Generally, optimization tasks are conducted a posteriori when the process is completed. It is the opposite to a proactive improvement.

Due to these limitations, especially 2., the datastream processing or Data Stream Mining (DSM) has become an emerging topic within the Big Data area [18,30]. A datastream is a digital representation and continuous transmission of data that describes a class of related events [9,23]. Through its processing, it is possible to achieve decision-making in real-time, i.e. when events occur. This opens up new and wide opportunities for value creation in organizations. Examples of these systems are banks, hospitals and shops, and their systems of public attention. The operation of Smart Grids or agriculture applications mediated by sensors are instances too. For agriculture applications, the generation of early warnings for the detection of diseases in crops such as the "Burning Rice" (Pyricularia oryzae) in the area of Entre Ríos is an adequate example.

In some organizations, the data are stored in their management systems which usually use database relational models. This model allows analytics elaboration but its implementation may be inappropriate because the performance is affected, especially in Software as a Service (SaaS) contexts. The system can collapse due to continuous queries to perform the monitoring. There are also organizations where data is generated in a distributed way through different devices: sensors, weather stations or GPS devices, without a centralized management system. For these reasons, the event generation and their processing as datastreams can constitute the base technology to enable efficient monitoring and decision-making. In the first systems, it would be a parallel component to the attention system, and in the second it would be the processing system itself.

Particularly, in this work, we focus on the vehicle routing problem (VRP) [3,6] with real-time information provision and re-routing. This is oriented to the search for an intelligent mobility paradigm. Urban logistics, waste collection, public transport, drivers, among others, are examples of VRP. In these cases, the datastreams are generated in a distributed way by each agent involved, and they can be processed in centralized or distributed form according to the chosen scheme and the available resources.

This paper aims to show a prescriptive analytic model to solve an instance of the VRP. The particular problem has the following characteristics: total or partial delivery of homogeneous commodities, restriction of vehicle capacity and uncertain demand. The solution proposes to use agents with parallel reinforcement learning.

This paper is organized as follows: the following section describes theoretical concepts involved. Sections 3 and 4 develop the main characteristics of our agent and an argument about its experimental behavior. Finally, conclusions and future works are presented.

2   Previous Concepts

For the outlined problem solution: Vehicle Routing and its different applications, we consider different concepts related to Computational Intelligence and High Performance Computing (HPC). This section describes the basic concepts involved in the development of this work.

2.1   Vehicle Routing Problem

The Traveling Salesman Problem (TSP) is one of the most interesting combinatorial optimization problems. Its original formulation was made in 1934 by Hassler Whitney [8]. The problem is: an agent must visit n customers located in interconnected cities forming a complete graph K_n. Each interconnection (network arcs) between two cities (network vertices) i, j has an associated weight or distance $d_{ij} \in \mathbb{R}_0^+$. The agent wants to travel the minimum possible total distance, visiting each customer exactly once and returning to the home city, i.e. he wants to find the Hamilton circuit of minimum length. This TSP is one of the first problem to be proven NP-hard [14]. Today, there are a lot of papers about its different variants and solutions [13].

The vehicle routing problem (VRP) is a more general version of TSP. Its main difference is to consider multiple vehicles in its routing model (See Fig. 1). i.e., there is a set of customers, geographically dispersed around a central depot and a homogeneous vehicle fleet [3,6]. VRP is about how to optimally serve all of its customers. Since its formulation in 1959, VR modeling has been one of the most widely addressed topics in the framework of operation research, industrial engineering, logistics, and transportation. In particular, this paper considers a VRP variant. It has the following characteristics:

– Homogeneous goods: the distributed goods or merchandise are homogeneous and divisible. Demands must be satisfied as much as possible for most customers.

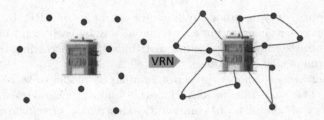

Fig. 1. Diagram of vehicle routing problem

- Vehicle capacity: All vehicles of the distribution fleet have a capacity that cannot be exceeded during each trip.
- Uncertain demand: the customers are distributed in the network and their demands are not known in advance, although estimates from predictive analytics might be available.
- Dynamic network conditions: during the operation stage, the travel times among delivery or replenishment locations may change due to various events, examples of them are traffic jams, street cuts for maintenance, and people mobilizations, among others. These changes are usually not known in advance, it is possible to sense the network status at any time and update all parameters.
- Stable customer portfolio: the customers and their location rarely vary over time.

Therefore, our variant VRP has a vehicular capacity(C) and uncertainty conditions(U), is dynamic(D) and real-time(RT). We call it RT-CUD-VRP.

2.2 Computational Intelligence

Computational Intelligence (CI; in some contexts, known as Soft Computing, SC) is a set of methodologies and approaches inspired by nature to address complex reality problems. CI differs from Hard Computing or conventional computing by its tolerance to imprecision, uncertainty, partial truth and approximation. Indeed, its model is the human mind and its guiding principle is to take advantage of imprecision, uncertainty, partial truth and approximation to achieve tractability, robustness and low-cost solutions. CI techniques include fuzzy logic, genetic algorithms, artificial neural networks, machine learning and expert systems [7,35]. These multiple methods are not competitive with each other, but they are complementary and can be used together to solve a given problem [26].

Within the CI field, the concept of learning and learning agents is our interest in the present work.

2.3 Agents and Their Learning

Learning is a process where the free parameters of a model are adapted through stimulation received from the environment that it is embedded in. The learning type is determined by how parameter changes occur [12]. A well-defined rule set for the learning problem solution is called a learning algorithm or training method. There is no single training algorithm, but a wide variety, and each one has its own advantages and disadvantages. Once a model has been trained by some learning algorithm and its free parameters are established, it is said the model .has learned and can perform tasks that it was trained for without its parameters being altered.

In [22], the learning agents are introduced. These can be designed with an action element (which decides what actions to carry out), and a learning element (to modify the action element and to improve the decision-making). The design of a learning element is mostly affected by three aspects:

- What components of the action item are to be learned.
- What feedback is available as learning input.
- What representation type is used for the components.

Each of these components can be learned through proper feedback. The learning's feedback type is usually the most important factor when the nature of the addressed learning problem is determined. Three types of learning are distinguished: supervised, unsupervised, and reinforcement learning.

Reinforcement learning is the most relevant in this context. An agent is able to judge and criticize its actions considering its perceptions and some measure of aptitude, reward, or reinforcement. The reinforcement learning task consists of using the observed rewards to learn an optimal (or near-optimal) policy from the environment [22], i.e., the one that maximizes the total rewards received from its interaction with the context. This policy tells the agent what to do in each possible state.

In a reinforcement learning system, it is possible to identify four main subelements: a policy, a reward signal, a value function, and, optionally, an environment model. Figure 2 shows each of them and their interactions. In [29], it is described each one of these elements as:

- A policy defines the behavior of a learning agent at a given time. It is a mapping from perceived states of the environment (each of which may be the observation O_t itself, or an internal representation periodically updated from it) to the actions (A_t) performed on those states. In some cases, the policy may be a simple function or lookup table, whereas in others it may involve extensive computation, e.g., a search process. In general, policies may be stochastic, they specify probabilities for each action.
- A reward signal R_t defines the reinforcement learning problem goal. At each time step, the environment sends to the agent a reward (it is a single number). The agent's objective is to maximize the total reward (return or value) received over the long run. In consequence, the reward signal defines which are

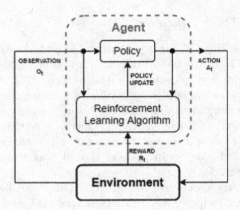

Fig. 2. Reinforcement learning process

the good and bad events for the agent. This is the primary basis for altering the policy: if an action implies a low reward, then the policy may be changed, and some other action is applied in the future to the same situation. In general, reward signals may be stochastic functions of the environment state and the actions taken.

- A value function specifies what is good in the long run. Generally, the value of a state is the total reward amount that an agent can expect to accumulate in the future if it starts from this state. Rewards are primary, whereas values, as predictions of rewards, are secondary. Nevertheless, action choices are made mostly based on value judgments rather than on immediate rewards.
- The final element of some reinforcement learning systems is an environment model. It mimics the behavior of the environment, or more generally, it allows making inferences over the environment's behavior. Models are used to plan, i.e. decide an action by considering possible future situations before they occur. Methods for solving reinforcement learning problems that use models and planning are called model-based methods. They are opposed to simple model-free methods which are trial-and-error learners, and generally, they are viewed as the contrary to planning.

Methods that learn approximations to both policy and value functions are often called $actor - critic$ methods. They learn approximations for policy ($actor$) and value function ($critic$). The policy is parameterized, and the learning algorithm adjusts them according to a stochastic gradient ascent rule while accumulating experience by interacting with the environment and getting observations and rewards [29]. Particularly, the Proximal Policy Optimization (PPO) family [25] follows this strategy. Besides, some member algorithms can apply high-performance computing (HPC) in GPU in order to speed up their response time. This property is very desirable by the high computational effort involved, especially during the training phase. In the next section, we refer to HPC.

2.4   High Performance Computing in GPU

In most cases, High Performance Computing (HPC) refers to adding computing power in such a way that higher performance is achieved than one could
get out in a typical PC or workstation. Generally, HPC is applied in computational solutions of large problems in science, engineering, or business. A Big
Data Systems is a particular case, it needs to process huge data volumes and,
consequently, demands greater computational capacity. For this reason, conventional computer systems are not suitable for proper processing. HPC techniques
allow intensive computational operations and improve processing speed; involv-
ing different technologies such as distributed and parallel systems [18,30].

Parallel programming explicitly breaks the task down into smaller units,
where each unit can be executed in parallel on a single processing core. Graphic
processing units (GPU) are a possible and cheap parallel device. Nowadays the
computational power of the GPU is used to solve any kind of problems, not
only of a graphic nature. This is known as GPGPU (GPU General Purpose
Computing) [15,33]. When the GPU is used as a parallel computer, the number of
processing units, the hybrid memory structure and the possible threads working
in parallel are taken into account. The CUDA programming model, developed
by NVIDIA, allows considering a GPU as a highly parallel computer, providing
a high-level programming environment. It defines a GPU as a programmable coprocessor of CPU [16,17,28]. This architecture is formed by multiple streaming
multiprocessors, each with several scalar processors. Many CUDA libraries have
been developed to solve typical problems. For example, for Machine Learning
(ML), TensorFlow is a good and emerging programming framework supporting
the execution of distributed applications on heterogeneous hardware [27].

TensorFlow is an open-source programming framework. Initially, it was
designed for developing ML applications, although its aim is to support the
development of a wide range of applications, including HPC applications, that
are outside the ML. There are different performance results that demonstrate
that TensorFlow is a good HPC programming framework.

By VRP's characteristics, it can hardly be addressed by exact methods (integer linear programming or dynamic programming) when its size is big, even
using the GPU computing power [19]. Nevertheless, the heuristic or metaheuris-
tic methods show improvements in response times by using different parallel
computational schemes [21].

Another issue is the loss of the optimal solution by variation in some problem
parameters. This involves determining a new solution taking into account the
current state. The changes can occur many times during the process, being
necessary to correct them in order not to incur losses or damages. The review
process implies less cost than initial planning, but repeated multiple times can
affect the online or real-time decision-making process.

Considering all detailed properties, we propose to solve the RT-CUD-VRP
by applying reinforcement learning with parallel techniques in GPU. In this
work, we use GPU, particularly CUDA, and TensorFlow to achieve the agents'
learning. The next section describes the proposed solution.

3 Prescriptive Model to RT-CUD-VRP

This paper presents a prescriptive analytics model for RT-CUD-VRP. The solution proposes the use of reinforcement learning agents applying parallel computation techniques in GPU in order to achieve training acceleration.

Given the characteristics of RT-CUD-VRP, we select an Actor-Critical agent using the Proximal Policy Optimization method (PPO) [25]. This algorithm alternates between the experience generation (stored as trajectories, through interaction with the environment) and the objective function optimization (by stochastic gradient ascent using the generated experience). This way of working accelerates training by generating several epochs of updates in mini-batches.

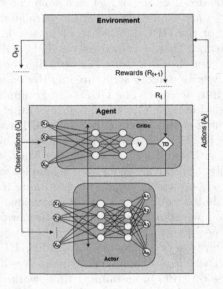

Fig. 3. Diagram of an PPO Actor-Critical agent

For this agent kind it is possible to use neural networks, one for the actor policy in order to project states into a probability distribution of actions, and another for the critic, who learns a value function for the current actor's policy. Figure 3 shows the agent diagram with both networks. Both networks receive from the environment an observation with multiple characteristics $(x_1, x_2, ..., x_n)$. It can be observed that both actor and critic do not directly access rewards signal and actions, respectively.

As described by [4,29], reinforcement learning methods have so far been applied to simple decision-making problems, mainly related to game solving, to states represented with fixed-dimensional matrices from image or sensor processing, and to basic decisions. The great challenge ahead is to adapt actor-critic methods to address an increasingly wide range of real-world problems of scientific and social importance. RL has the potential to improve the quality, efficiency and cost-effectiveness of the processes on which we depend in education, healthcare, transportation and energy management, among others. To achieve this, the design decisions and adjustments involved in implementing RL must be addressed. The architecture has to be designed by selecting appropriate learning algorithms, state and action representations, training procedures, hyperparameter settings, and other design details [4].

In order to solve RT-CUD-VRP using the PPO algorithm, we design the environment, observations, actions, rewards, and functions of value and policy with their training algorithms, below we describe each of them.

3.1 Environment

A dynamic simulated environment was set. Such environment has information about customers' locations, travel times and uncertain demand models in the form of fuzzy numbers. Each vehicle has a capacity that cannot be surpassed. Also, the environment is in charge of keeping track of time spent and overall demand met. The environment keeps a 'travel log'. Each vehicle follows the process flow shown in Fig. 4, generating different events for each transition. Each event is a decision instance where the agent has to select a proper action.

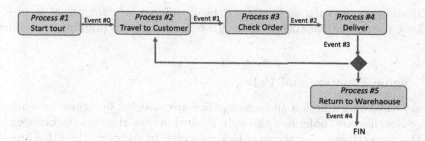

Fig. 4. Diagram of a PPO Actor-Critical agent

3.2 Agent Actions

Depending on the state the environment is in, the agent can make one of the following decisions (actions):

- How many products to deliver to a customer. At the visit moment, the client can order an arbitrary amount. In this situation, the agent has to decide: not to deliver, to deliver only half of requested, or to deliver all requests.
- The next destination. The tour starts with initial planning, but at the beginning or after visiting a customer, the agent decides who the next client to visit, or return to the warehouse and end the trip.

3.3   Observations

From the environment interaction, in each time step, the agent receives an observation composed by:

- Current customer number.
- Current time from tour start.
- Merchandise available.
- Customer order: required product quantity by the current customer. This quantity may be greater or less than initially estimated.

From this observation, the agent can determine the next action to take.

3.4   Rewards

The reward signal defines the objective that the agent tries to accomplish. The agent can receive a reward signal R_t at every time step t, when ending each tour. In our case, the reward signal returned at the end of the trip is composed by:

- Customer satisfaction metric: It is a numerical value that represents the fulfillment level of customers' expectations about the relationship between their orders and what is delivered to them.
- Total travel time.

In addition, at each step of the trip, a different reward signal is used to reinforce instant actions such as visiting a new customer or fulfilling a customer's order.

3.5   Value Function and Policy

As said, the value function and agent policy are modeled by neural networks. In both cases they are configured through received inputs, they are the observations and the respective specifications of hidden layers. In addition, the value function neural network receives as parameters an activation function for the output layer (usually Tanh or ReLU functions [5] are used). While the network of the policy receives an activation function and the specifications of the possible actions to generate by the output layer. This layer produces a probability distribution on actions.

In the next section, we detail the main characteristics of implementation and its experimental results.

4   Experimental Study

The proposed model is developed in the Python language version 3.7, with library management and their configurations through Anaconda [2, 10]. Jupyter Notebook with its documents .ipynb is used as development environment [31, 34]. It allows us to combine elements of different nature.

The reinforcement learning agent was developed with TensorFlow APIs. Within its ecosystem, we mainly use TF-Agents [1, 11, 27]. It provides a paradigm for the design, implementation and testing of parallel reinforcement learning agents.

For RT-CUD-VRP integration into a dynamic and complex environment, a system simulation was developed through the Simpy library. Several instances were designed as a form of initial validation and with the aim of showing model's strengths and weaknesses.

The base instance is conformed by 9 clients and a single depot. The requirements in each client are modeled in the environment by fuzzy trapezoidal numbers, and the unloading times by triangular ones. In the simulation, these numbers are sampled to generate different possible instances, as suggested in [20, 32]. Besides, each travel time was considered deterministic and dynamic. Each of the instances is described as:

LuSi. Low-uncertainty static instance: We parameterized the base instance with near-deterministic demands and unloading times. All demands were set to (40, 43, 46, 50) unities and unloading times to (0.3,0.4,0.45) minutes by unity.

LuDi. Low-uncertainty dynamic instance: Next, a second instance was configured with near-deterministic demands and unloading times, but the travel times change during the simulation. The changes are intended to reflect differences in travel times during peak hours. Selected routes leading downtown were multiplied by a factor of 4, and the remaining by 1.5.

HuDi. High-uncertainty dynamic instance: Finally, the last instance was configured to consider more uncertainty in the demands and unloading times. Also, the dynamic changes described in the previous instance were kept. The parameters used were (30, 45, 55, 75) for the demands and (0.3, 0.7, 2.0) for the unloading times.

In order to make fair comparisons, the same architecture for actor and critic networks was used in all simulations. An input dense layer with 8 neurons, a hidden LSTM layer with 16 neurons and an output dense layer with 4 neurons for the critic network. An input dense layer with 8 neurons, a hidden LSTM layer with 26 neurons and an output dense layer with 13 neurons for the actor. The LSTM type was selected because of the decision process' sequential nature.

The platform used for the execution of the experiments is a notebook with an "Intel(R) Core(TM) i7-7700HQ CPU @ 2.80 GHz 2.81 GHz" processor, 16 GB of RAM and a "NVIDIA GeForce GTX 1050 Ti" GPU with 4 GB of GDDR5 dedicated RAM, with Windows 10×64 operating system. The developed code is available at [24].

As can be seen in Fig. 5, the agent achieves learning in all three instances. The figures show the average performance of the agent policy on each instance after n training steps. We observe that the maximum possible return achievable is approximately 600 in LuSi instance. This value is reached by the agent towards the end of training.

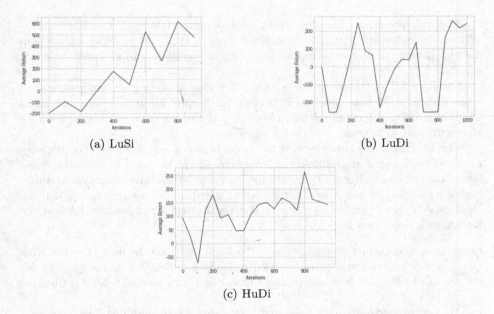

(a) LuSi

(b) LuDi

(c) HuDi

Fig. 5. Average return of policy trained in three instance

When facing LuDi and HuDi instances, the agent has more trouble to reach overall high returns, and it can be seen that as uncertainty increases, the overall performance decreases. However, the agent learns a policy that achieves satisfactory results. It is expected that a more descriptive state can help to improve the agent's performance. Furthermore, this *needs* to be done in order to achieve a generalizable and incremental model if the stable customer portfolio assumption does not hold.

5   Conclusions and Future Works

In this work, we propose a solution to a Vehicle Routing Problem instance: RT-CUD-VRP. Its characteristics are total or partial delivery of homogeneous commodities, vehicle capacity restriction, uncertainty conditions, dynamic, and real-time. The proposal uses intelligent agents with GPU parallel reinforcement learning. We describe a prescriptive analytic model and each of its components. Besides the main implementation details in open source are mentioned.

The experimental analysis shows the agent can learn a policy that performs sufficiently well in three designed cases, exhibiting strengths and weaknesses of model. The initial results are encouraging and motivate further works.

As future lines, it is hoped to develop a comprehensive analysis of the proposal through a thorough experimental check. It is also intended to extend the model to solve any variant of dynamic VRP in real-time. Such generalization will require a universal representation of the states, having to explorer techniques of graph embeddings. Finally, we want to validate the our solution in other problems with the same nature of VRP. Respect the computational performance, we have to do a comparative evaluation with other solutions, with or without HPC.

References

1. Abadi, M., et al.: TensorFlow: a system for large-scale machine learning. In: OSDI, vol. 16, pp. 265–283 (2016)
2. Anaconda: Anaconda documentation (2022). https://www.anaconda.com/products
3. Asghari, M., Mirzapour Al-e-hashem, S.M.J.: Green vehicle routing problem: a state-of-the-art review. Int. J. Prod. Econ. **231**, 107899 (2021). https://doi.org/10.1016/j.ijpe.2020.107899. https://www.sciencedirect.com/science/article/pii/S0925527320302607
4. Barto, A.G., Sutton, R.S., Anderson, C.W.: Looking back on the actor-critic architecture. IEEE Trans. Syst. Man Cybern. Syst. **51**(1), 40–50 (2021). https://doi.org/10.1109/TSMC.2020.3041775
5. Borrero, I., Arias, M.: Deep Learning. Alonso Barba, Universidad de Huelva (2021). https://books.google.com.ar/books?id=kzsvEAAAQBAJ
6. Clarke, G., Wright, J.W.: Scheduling of vehicles from a central depot to a number of delivery points. Oper. Res. **12**(4), 568–581 (1964). http://www.jstor.org/stable/167703
7. Ebrahimnejad, A., Verdegay, J.L.: Fuzzy Sets-Based Methods and Techniques for Modern Analytics. SFSC, vol. 364. Springer, Cham (2018). https://doi.org/10.1007/978-3-319-73903-8
8. Flood, M.M.: The traveling-salesman problem. Oper. Res. **4**(1), 61–75 (1956). http://www.jstor.org/stable/167517
9. Garofalakis, M., Gehrke, J., Rastogi, R.: Data Stream Management: Processing High-Speed Data Streams. Data-Centric Systems and Applications. Springer, Heidelberg (2016). https://doi.org/10.1007/978-3-540-28608-0. https://books.google.com.ar/books?id=qiSpDAAAQBAJ
10. Gorelick, M., Ozsvald, I.: High Performance Python: Practical Performant Programming for Humans. O'Reilly Media (2020). https://books.google.com.ar/books?id=kKjgDwAAQBAJ
11. Hafner, D., Davidson, J., Vanhoucke, V.: TensorFlow agents: efficient batched reinforcement learning in TensorFlow. CoRR abs/1709.02878 (2017). http://arxiv.org/abs/1709.02878
12. Haykin, S.: Neural Networks: A Comprehensive Foundation. Macmillan, New York (1994)
13. Huerta, I.I., Neira, D.A., Ortega, D.A., Varas, V., Godoy, J., Asín-Achá, R.: Improving the state-of-the-art in the traveling salesman problem: an anytime automatic algorithm selection. Expert Syst. Appl. **187**, 115948 (2022). https://doi.org/10.1016/j.eswa.2021.115948. https://www.sciencedirect.com/science/article/pii/S0957417421013014
14. Karp, R.M.: Reducibility among Combinatorial Problems, pp. 85–103. Springer, Boston (1972). https://doi.org/10.1007/978-1-4684-2001-2_9
15. Kirk, D., Hwu, W.: Programming Massively Parallel Processors: A Hands-on Approach. Elsevier Science (2016)

16. NVIDIA: NVIDIA CUDA Compute Unified Device Architecture, Programming Guide. NVIDIA (2020)
17. NVIDIA: Nvidia: CUDA C++ Programming Guide, Design Guide. NVIDIA (2021)
18. Pacheco, P., Malensek, M.: An Introduction to Parallel Programming. Elsevier Science (2021). https://books.google.com.ar/books?id=rElkCwAAQBAJ
19. Perumalla, K., Alam, M.: Design considerations for GPU-based mixed integer programming on parallel computing platforms, chap. 27. Association for Computing Machinery, New York (2021). https://doi.org/10.1145/3458744.3473366
20. Pulido-López, D.G., García, M., Figueroa-García, J.C.: Fuzzy uncertainty in random variable generation: a cumulative membership function approach. In: Figueroa-García, J.C., López-Santana, E.R., Villa-Ramírez, J.L., Ferro-Escobar, R. (eds.) WEA 2017. CCIS, vol. 742, pp. 398–407. Springer, Cham (2017). https://doi.org/10.1007/978-3-319-66963-2_36
21. Rashid, M.H., McAndrew, I.: An efficient GPU framework for parallelizing combinatorial optimization heuristics. In: 2020 International Conference on Advances in Computing and Communication Engineering (ICACCE), pp. 1–7 (2020). https://doi.org/10.1109/ICACCE49060.2020.9155072
22. Russell, S.J., Norvig, P.: Inteligencia artificial: un enfoque moderno. Pearson Prentice Hall, Madrid (2004)
23. Rutkowski, L., Jaworski, M., Duda, P.: Stream Data Mining: Algorithms and Their Probabilistic Properties. SBD, vol. 56. Springer, Cham (2020). https://doi.org/10.1007/978-3-030-13962-9. https://books.google.com.ar/books?id=P0-NDwAAQBAJ
24. Schab, E.A., Casanova, C.A., Piccoli, M.F.: Reinforcement learning for VRP, April 2022. https://github.com/estebanschab/RL-VRP
25. Schulman, J., Wolski, F., Dhariwal, P., Radford, A., Klimov, O.: Proximal policy optimization algorithms (2017). arXiv preprint arXiv:1707.06347
26. Siddique, N., Adeli, H.: Computational Intelligence: Synergies of Fuzzy Logic, Neural Networks and Evolutionary Computing. Wiley (2013). https://books.google.com.ar/books?id=CbpbuA0jvVgC
27. Singh, P., Manure, A.: Learn TensorFlow 2.0: Implement Machine Learning and Deep Learning Models with Python. Apress (2019). https://books.google.com.ar/books?id=3_rEDwAAQBAJ
28. Soyata, T.: GPU Parallel Program Development Using CUDA. T. Francis, Abingdon (2018)
29. Sutton, R., Barto, A.: Reinforcement Learning: An Introduction. MIT Press (2018)
30. Terzo, O., Martinovič, J.: HPC, Big Data, and AI Convergence Towards Exascale: Challenge and Vision. CRC Press (2022). https://books.google.com.ar/books?id=2NpXEAAAQBAJ
31. Toomey, D.: Learning Jupyter 5: Explore Interactive Computing Using Python, Java, JavaScript, R, Julia, and JupyterLab, 2nd edn. Packt Publishing (2018). https://books.google.com.ar/books?id=8kZsDwAAQBAJ
32. Varón-Gaviria, C.A., Barbosa-Fontecha, J.L., Figueroa-García, J.C.: Fuzzy uncertainty in random variable generation: an α-cut approach. In: Huang, D.-S., Hussain, A., Han, K., Gromiha, M.M. (eds.) ICIC 2017. LNCS (LNAI), vol. 10363, pp. 264–273. Springer, Cham (2017). https://doi.org/10.1007/978-3-319-63315-2_23

33. Wilt, N.: The CUDA Handbook: A Comprehensive Guide to GPU Programming. Addison Wesley (2020). https://books.google.com.ar/books?id=lUVQswEACAAJ

34. Wintjen, M., Vlahutin, A.: Practical Data Analysis Using Jupyter Notebook: Learn How to Speak the Language of Data by Extracting Useful and Actionable Insights Using Python. Packt Publishing (2020). https://books.google.com. ar/books?id=tqTsDwAAQBAJ

35. Zadeh, L.A.: Fuzzy logic, neural networks, and soft computing. Commun. ACM **37**(3), 77–84 (1994). https://doi.org/10.1145/175247.175255

Virtual Reality

A Cross-Platform Immersive 3D Environment for Algorithm Learning

Sebastián Dapoto[1]([✉]) [ID], Federico Cristina[1] [ID], Gamal Lascano[2], Pablo Thomas[1] [ID], and Patricia Pesado[1] [ID]

[1] III-LIDI, Universidad Nacional de La Plata, La Plata, Buenos Aires, Argentina
{sdapoto,fcristina,pthomas,ppesado}@lidi.info.unlp.edu.ar
[2] Facultad de Informática, Universidad Nacional de La Plata, La Plata, Buenos Aires, Argentina

Abstract. The educational field must adapt itself to changes and new ways of learning. M-learning proposes modern methods of supporting the learning process through the use of mobile devices that allow students to access study tools and materials at any time and place. In particular, in the initial levels of computer science careers, these types of tools facilitate the construction of knowledge and develop students' ability to solve problems, using flexible platforms that promote self-learning. The development of mobile applications with three-dimensional (3D) environments that make use of virtual reality, increase the interest of students in the use of learning support tools, and encourage the resolution of the proposed problems. This paper presents a novel 3D mobile application with virtual reality to support the learning of basic algorithms.

Keywords: M-learning · 3D mobile applications · Virtual reality · Unity · Basic algorithm learning

1 Introduction

Nowadays, mobile devices have become one of the most essential objects in people's daily lives. These devices are not only used as a communication or entertainment tool, but are also very important for academic or work tasks. In addition, the constant evolution of mobile devices provides more and more computing capacity and, therefore, allows the execution of more complex applications.

M-learning is the evolution of e-learning and proposes the use of the potential of mobile devices in teaching and learning processes. Thus, learning becomes a personalized, portable, cooperative and interactive activity, adding a new dimension to the traditional education system [1].

M-learning offers complete flexibility for students, making it possible to select the content they wish to see, at the chosen time and place. The contents should not be dependent on a particular device and should be adaptable to the characteristics of each device, taking into account the navigability, processing capacity and connection speed they have.

E. Rucci et al. (Eds.): JCC-BD&ET 2022, CCIS 1634, pp. 125–138, 2022.
https://doi.org/10.1007/978-3-031-14599-5_9

Software development for M-Learning is a complex process that requires a balanced management of requirements during their elicitation, analysis, specification and prioritization, in order to subsequently design and code the application. There is a set of basic requirements that are important to capture during the elicitation process, such as the existing mobile computing infrastructure, the instructional level and type of learning, the human-mobile interaction, the evolution of learning content and software, among others [2].

On the other hand, applications that have a three-dimensional environment are vi-sually more pleasing and generate a greater attraction in the users who use them. This occurs mainly because simulated 3D environments are closer to reality than two-dimensional environments, allowing the user to engage more actively with the environment [3]. If an application offers, in addition, Virtual Reality (VR) functionality, the user experience is further enriched [4].

VR is an interactive computer simulation in which the real world is replaced with sensory information received by the user. A VR system has three basic elements [5]:

- Interactive simulation: the user's actions directly affect the images displayed. The VR system responds in real time.
- Implicit interaction: it is not necessary for the user to explicitly communicate the will to perform an action. The system captures the user's will implicitly in their natural movements. The clearest example of this is the virtual reality system's camera control, which is updated based on the user's head movements.
- Sensory immersion: sensory immersion is the disconnection of the senses from the real world and connection to the virtual world. The user ceases to perceive the surrounding environment and becomes immersed in the virtual world recreated by the computer in real time.

M-learning applications that use three-dimensional environments and contain Virtual Reality functionality increase the interest of students in the use of support tools, and encourage the resolution of the problems posed in learning. This work proposes a 3D Mobile Application with Virtual Reality, which serves as a support for the learning of basic algorithms in the initial subjects of the careers of the Facultad de Informática of the Universidad Nacional de La Plata.

This work presents a novel 3D mobile application with virtual reality to support the learning of basic algorithms. The rest of the paper is organized as follows: Section 2 presents related work; Sect. 3 describes the motivation; Sect. 4 presents details of the development of the mobile application, Sect. 5 shows the results obtained and Sect. 6 presents the conclusions; finally, Sect. 7 presents future work.

2   Related Works

Currently there are several software alternatives dedicated to teaching different programming language paradigms. Codecraft [6] is an educational desktop video game that attempts to teach the fundamentals of computer programming to children between the ages of 6 and 18. Another well-known desktop application is Alice [7], a three-dimensional learning environment for teaching computer programming concepts to beginning students. In [8], a game-based learning model of 3D computer programming and computational problem solving for computer science students is presented. A method for planning and executing object-oriented programming learning activities supported by digital modeling and fabrication is presented in [9]. A 3D visualization tool called OOPVisual, which simulates object-oriented programming concepts to aid students in their understanding, is shown in [10]. [11] presents a project named Cubely, an immersive VR programming environment in which novice programmers solve programming puzzles within a virtual world. The solutions to the exercises are assembled by the programmer within the same virtual world using the cubes representing program instructions. The research presented in [12] uses a simple, student-centered virtual environment to teach programming concepts, making learning interactive and fun.

On the digital distribution platform of mobile applications Google Play [13] for devices with Android operating system it is possible to find a wide variety of mobile applications for learning programming languages. The same happens on the Apple App Store platform [14], which allows users to search and download applications developed for the iOS operating system. Some of the applications found on both platforms are: Mimo [15], Sololearn [16], Grasshopper [17], Programming Hub [18], among others.

In this section we have listed the works related to tools for learning programming concepts. Some research works have been found with tools for teaching programming in 3D environments, however, none of them are prepared to be used on a mobile device. In addition, no tools have been found that use 3D and VR environments to teach basic programming concepts including concurrent programming concepts and paralle-lism. On the other hand, in the search performed in the distribution sites for Android and iOS mobile operating systems, the applications found are focused on learning one or several programming languages in particular, and none of them has a three-dimensional environment or the possibility of using virtual reality.

3   Motivation

The concepts to be included in the initial levels of computer science and related careers, generate a favorable scenario to create tools that support the characteristics proposed by m-learning.

In particular, a software tool called R-Info is used in the entry course of the Facul-tad de Informática of the Universidad Nacional de La Plata for learning the basic concepts of algorithm construction [19–21]. Through the use of this desktop tool, students can create algorithms of simple and medium complexity and visualize the execution of these algorithms. That is, the tool allows them to solve problems in a visual environment.

Nowadays, most of the students starting computer science careers have a mobile device, which they have included in their daily lives. These students prefer to have the support material directly on their devices, instead of carrying them in physical form. A clear example of this is that they do not usually have the practical work guides printed, but use them directly from their mobile device. This is mainly due to the versatility it gives students, having all the learning support material at any time and place, without having to carry physical objects.

In order to use the R-Info application, it is necessary to have a desktop computer. For many students, access to this type of equipment is not simple and is less conve-nient.

With this in mind, it is very convenient to have a mobile version of tools that support learning, such as R-Info, in order to encourage their use.

In the specific case of R-Info, it is possible to add more potential to the mobile version by substantially improving the visualization of the robot and the tasks it performs within the city. This is possible by developing a 3D graphical interface that transforms the new version into a more visually appealing, interesting and user-friendly tool [22, 23]. In addition, in order to provide an even more interactive experience to students, it is possible to add virtual reality functionality to the application. Thus, by using virtual reality glasses, the environment becomes immersive and allows the student to see the robot's actions as if he/she were performing them in first person.

Since the survey conducted in Sect. 2 did not find any tools with the characteristics mentioned in the previous paragraph, the idea arises to develop a 3D mobile version of R-Info, which allows teaching the basic concepts of programming, concurrency and parallelism, which is attractive and can be used with VR glasses to allow greater immersion in the three-dimensional environment.

3.1   R-Info

R-Info is a simple abstract machine, with a mobile robot controlled by a reduced set of primitive instructions, which allows modeling paths and tasks within a city formed by 100 streets (horizontal arteries) and 100 avenues (vertical arteries).

The main capabilities of the robot are:

- Advancing forward 1 block.
- Orienting itself to the right.
- Recognizing two types of objects, flowers and papers, which are located in the corners of the city.
- Picking up and/or placing flowers and papers on a corner (one at a time). Transporting these flowers and papers (the robot has a bag with unlimited capacity).
- Positioning directly in any corner of the city.
- Performing simple calculations, including variables if necessary.
- Using control structures, such as "while" or "repeat".
- Reporting the results obtained.

In addition, R-Info allows to define several robots, synchronize them, and define areas within the city, either shared or private, among other parallelism functionalities.

The main screen of the R-Info application has a control panel that allows, among other functions, to write the algorithm code and then execute it. In addition, the tool allows editing the state of the city (adding flowers and/or papers) and visualizing a portion of the city.

The left side of Fig. 1 shows the panel controls and the algorithm code. The right side of the figure shows the path taken by the robot according to the execution of the aforementioned algorithm. This path moves the robot from the corner (1, 1) to the corner (3, 2). As can be seen in Fig. 1, it is also possible to see the corners that have a flower (in red) and/or paper.

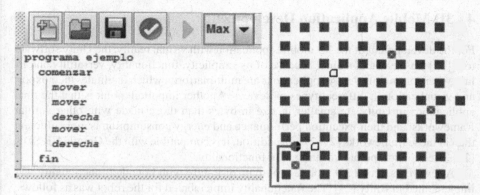

Fig. 1. R-Info application. (Color figure online)

R-Info also has the ability to create and instruct more than one robot. In this way, the designated robots perform the tasks simultaneously. In Fig. 2 it is possible to observe the result of the execution of an algorithm where several robots are used and there are flowers and papers in several corners of the city. It is possible to see the path taken by each of the robots involved.

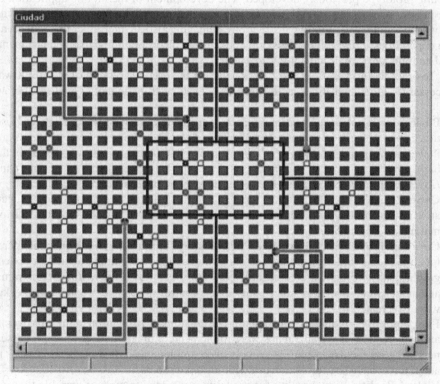

Fig. 2. Execution of an algorithm using several robots in parallel.

4   3D Mobile Application Development

For the development of the 3D mobile application with virtual reality, the Unity software tool [24] was selected, mainly because of its simplicity, functionality, versatility and its large user community. Unity applications are multiplatform, which facilitates their export and visualization in different types of devices. Another important point is that the final applications in Unity are smaller in size in bytes than those made with other similar frameworks, and their execution performance and energy consumption is more efficient than in those frameworks [25–27]. In addition, it is compatible with the Google VR SDK [28], used to incorporate virtual reality functionality.

A few years ago, a 3D mobile prototype of R-Info with bounded functionality was implemented in Unity [29]. The functionality implemented for the robot was as follows:

- Moving around the city.
- Transporting directly to a corner.
- Picking up and dropping off flowers and papers.
- Reporting messages on the screen.

In Fig. 3 it is possible to observe the robot performing tasks in the city in the 3D mobile prototype previously developed. The development of the mobile application of the present work is based on this prototype, and substantially extends the functionality by incorporating new primitive instructions, achieving also an interpreter that reflects all the capabilities of the original desktop application, incorporating visual enhancements and an immersive environment through VR.

In order to cover most of the functionality of the original version of R-Info, it was necessary to implement different features. The developed functionalities are listed below.

- **Basic functionalities**. Basic commands were added, such as *PosCa* (street position), *PosAv* (avenue position), *HayFlorEnLaEsquina* (returns if there is at least one flower in the corner), *HayFlorEnLaBolsa* (returns if there is at least one flower in the bag), *HayPapelEnLaEsquina* (returns if there is at least one paper in the corner) and *HayPapel-EnLaBolsa* (returns if there is at least one paper in the bag).
- **Control structures**. The different types of control structures were implemented, iterative ones such as *repetir* (repeat) and *mientras* (while), and the structure for decision making *Si* (if) and *Sino* (else).
- **Core functionalities**. The necessary functionality for the use of mathematical operators, the use of variables and the nesting of instructions were implemented. A lexicographic analyzer was also created, necessary to verify errors in the writing of programs, and an indentation identifier, necessary to use control structures. A condition checker was also created.
- **Functionalities related to parallelism**. The creation and execution of multiple robots and the creation of variable maps were implemented. In addition, parallel processes, necessary for the use of multiple robots, were implemented. It was also necessary to adapt the control structures to work with multiple robots.
- **Virtual Reality**. Virtual reality functionality was added to make it possible to use it with VR glasses, achieving an immersive environment.

- **Desktop version**. Since Unity is multiplatform, a desktop version (Mac OS/Linux/Windows) was also created. For this it was necessary to make an adaptation of the interface, including a special functionality that allows opening and saving source code files.

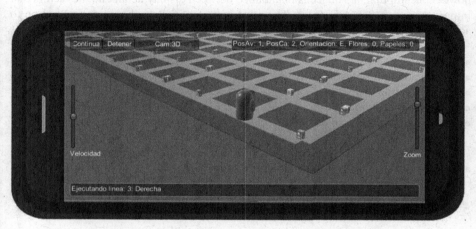

Fig. 3. R-Info 3D mobile prototype with bounded functionality.

In addition to the functionalities listed above, some visual features were developed to make the visualization of the tasks performed by the robot over the city more attractive. Among the visual functionalities that the application has, the following can be mentioned:

- **Selection between different 3D views**. Since the application presents a three-dimensional environment, the city and the objects within it can be observed from different points of view. It is possible to choose between three different predefined views: 1st person, 3rd person, aerial view.
- **Scene zoom adjustment**. In all views it is possible to adjust the zoom level to zoom in or out of the scene.
- **Horizontal panning of the scene**. This feature allows a rotation of the current view, to make possible the visualization of other sectors of the city.
- **Execution speed regulation**. It is possible to regulate the execution speed of the algorithm, and thus visualize the actions performed by the robot in the city with less or more speed.
- **Language selection**. It is possible to choose between Spanish or English.
- **On-screen information**. There is the possibility of displaying text messages on the screen.
- **Virtual reality display mode**. As an alternative to the three available display modes, it is possible to select the VR mode. To use this mode, VR glasses or lenses are required, as the screen is divided in the middle into two small screens, one for each eye.

When executing an algorithm, it is possible to run it from start to finish or to perform a step-by-step execution. At any time it is possible to stop the execution or res-tart it.

Another aspect that was taken into account was that the application should be supported by the widest possible spectrum of mobile devices in terms of computational capacity. In addition, the use of the application should not affect the daily use of the devices.

In order to maintain adequate execution performance and minimize the application's power consumption, a balance is maintained between display detail and the factors that impact these two items the most. The most important factors that were focused on to achieve this balance were [25, 26]:

- Number of objects in scene.
- Total amount of polygons to render.
- Use of lighting and shadow casting.
- Texture application.
- Animation of objects in scene.

The following section presents the results obtained, showing in detail the 3D mobile application and the different functionalities developed.

5 Results

The 3D VR mobile application is intended to provide a software tool that has the functionality of the original R-Info application, but is much more attractive and has greater flexibility, being able to be used anytime, anywhere.

The visual interface is fully three-dimensional and allows a choice of different viewpoints. Figure 4 shows the algorithm editing module of the application. Through this panel it is possible to write the code of the algorithm to be executed.

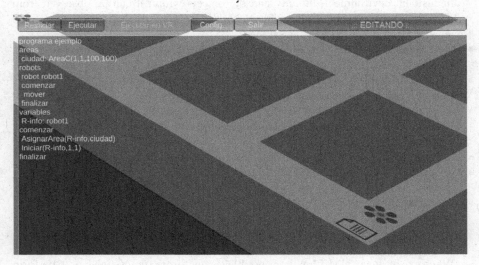

Fig. 4. Code edition panel.

In Fig. 5 it is possible to observe an algorithm in execution. In this case, the third person view is being used. In the upper part of the screen it is possible to observe the information about the position of the robot, its orientation, the number of flowers and papers that the robot has and the number of flowers and papers that exist in the corner where the robot is positioned. At the bottom is displayed the current state of execution of the algorithm, i.e., the current instruction or the completed state. The zoom level and speed are configurable via the side bar controls. There is also a bar control at the bottom, by means of which it is possible to change the perspective point of the view.

Figure 6 shows the first-person view. There is also a third alternative available, which allows the city to be viewed from an aerial position.

Additionally, a Virtual Reality mode was incorporated, for which it was necessary to use the Google VR API [28]. This mode allows the execution of the algorithm from an immersive view, where the user becomes the robot.

The API used includes a crosshair pointer that allows interacting with the environment. By adding a timer component to this pointer system, it was possible to interact with the elements when they are pointed at for a small period of time. In this way it is possible to control the application when it is in VR execution mode, without the need to interact with the screen in a tactile way. For example, if you point on a button for a brief moment, you are indicating that you want to press that button.

The VR algorithm execution mode has a different interface created specifically for this functionality. As can be seen in Fig. 7, the screen is divided into two parts, one for each eye, to make it possible to use it through the VR glasses. Three panels were implemented: a first panel to start the execution of the algorithm, a second panel to accept the messages created by the *Informar* (report) command, and a last panel to return to the normal mode of the application, i.e., the non-VR mode.

Fig. 5. Execution panel. Third person view.

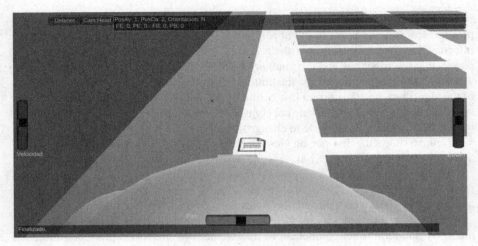

Fig. 6. Execution panel. First person view.

Since the VR run mode must be used through specific glasses, this functionality is not available in the desktop version of the application.

The desktop version contains a slightly different interface than the one used in the mobile application. The option to open and save source code files has been added, using Unity Standalone File Browser [30], since Unity does not support the functionality to open and save files using the native UI of the host operating system. In addition, the possibility of resizing the window from the window axes has been added, in conjunction with a resolution selector. In Fig. 8 it is possible to observe the desktop version of the application.

Fig. 7. Virtual reality mode of use.

The 3D mobile application developed was used by a set of 10 students with mid-range mobile devices. The experience of use was mostly positive. The positive aspects stated by the students were related to the 3D environment, the visualization of the animations related to the actions performed by the robot in the city and the possibility of using the immersive VR environment. As a point for improvement, in some devices with lower computational capacity, the application lost fluidity during the rendering of the robot's animations.

Fig. 8. Desktop version of the application.

6 Conclusions

A multiplatform immersive 3D environment was developed to support the learning of basic algorithms in the initial levels of computer science careers. The functionality of the original desktop version was covered, adding control structures, mathematical operators, variables, multiple robots, variable maps and parallelism, among others.

Since it is a mobile application, it motivates and facilitates the student's task of understanding the basic concepts of algorithms, since it allows performing algorithm execution tests wherever the student is. This provides total flexibility with respect to time and place of use.

The 3D environment is an additional attraction for students to be interested in u-sing the application. Through the different points of view, it allows a better visualization of the tasks performed by the robot over the city, strengthening their experience in the visualization of the executed algorithms.

A specific interface was developed to use the application with VR glasses. The possibility of using this visualization mode provides greater versatility, increasing the sense of immersion and stimulating the use of the application.

Being a multiplatform application, it was possible to create a desktop version for those students who wish to make use of this platform. This version contains a slightly different interface than the mobile version, allowing, for example, the choice of window size, and also has the option to open and save source code files.

Since no similar applications have been found, the 3D mobile application with virtual reality developed is considered a contribution to the teaching of basic algorithms in the initiation to programming, in a university degree in Computer Science. The application tries to improve the student's experience, becoming a very useful tool in their task of learning basic algorithms.

7   Future Works

One of the possible improvements to be made is to reform the lexicographic analyzer, to provide greater detail when reporting an error.

In addition, visual improvements are planned for the 3D mobile application, such as a quality selector in video rendering, selection of different types of robots, visual and sound effects in the animations, among others.

As a main objective, it is intended that the 3D mobile application will be massively used in the subjects of the entrance course of the different careers of the Facultad de Informática of the Universidad Nacional de La Plata, which are taught at different times throughout the year.

References

1. Khan, A., Al-Khanjari, Z.A., Sarrab, M.: Integrated design model for mobile learning pedagogy and application. J. Appl. Res. Technol. **16**(2), 146–159 (2018). https://doi.org/10.22201/icat.16656423.2018.16.2.709
2. Khan, A.I., Al-Khanjari, Z., Sarrab, M., Al-Shihi, H.: Generic requirements for M-learning software development. In: 2016 International Conference on Computational Techniques in Information and Communication Technologies (ICCTICT), pp. 192–195 (2016). https://doi.org/10.1109/ICCTICT.2016.7514577
3. Martin-Dorta, N., Sanchez-Berriel, I., Bravo, M., Hernandez, J., Saorin, J.L., Contero, M.: A 3D educational mobile game to enhance student's spatial skills. In: 2010 10th IEEE International Conference on Advanced Learning Technologies, pp. 6–10 (2010). https://doi.org/10.1109/ICALT.2010.9
4. Mesároš, P., Mačková, D., Spišáková, M., Mandičák, T., Behúnová, A.: M-learning tool for modeling the building site parameters in mixed reality environment. In: 2016 International Conference on Emerging eLearning Technologies and Applications (ICETA), pp. 211–216 (2016). https://doi.org/10.1109/ICETA.2016.7802094
5. Avilés, D.G., Reinoso, A.S.: Desarrollo de una aplicación interactiva para la implementación de realidad virtual utilizando cascos de inmersión que facilite el aprendizaje sobre educación vial para personas que poseen licencia de conducir en la ciudad de Guayaquil. Trabajo final para la obtención del título de Ingeniero en Producción y Dirección en Artes Multimedia, Universidad Católica de Santiago de Guayaquil, Ecuador (2015)
6. Ventura, M., Ventura, J., Baker, C., Viklund, G., Roth, R., Broughman, J.: Development of a video game that teaches the fundamentals of computer programming. In: SoutheastCon 2015, pp. 1–5 (2015). https://doi.org/10.1109/SECON.2015.7133047
7. Alice. https://www.alice.org

8. Hong, T., Chu, H.: Effects of a situated 3D computational problem-solving and programming game-based learning model on students' learning perception and cognitive loads. In: 2017 6th IIAI International Congress on Advanced Applied Informatics (IIAI-AAI), pp. 596–600 (2017). https://doi.org/10.1109/IIAI-AAI.2017.96
9. Oliveira, G.A.S., Bonacin, R.: A method for teaching object-oriented programming with digital modelling. In: 2018 IEEE 18th International Conference on Advanced Learning Technologies (ICALT), pp. 233–237 (2018). https://doi.org/10.1109/ICALT.2018.00060
10. Moussa, W.E., Almalki, R.M., Alamoudi, M.A., Allinjawi, A.: Proposing a 3D interactive visualization tool for learning OOP concepts. In: 2016 13th Learning and Technology Conference (L&T), pp. 1–7 (2016). https://doi.org/10.1109/LT.2016.7562861
11. Vincur, J., Konopka, M., Tvarozek, J., Hoang, M., Navrat, P.: Cubely: virtual reality block-based programming environment. In: Proceedings of the 23rd ACM Symposium on Virtual Reality Software and Technology (VRST 2017), pp. 1–2. Association for Computing Machinery, New York (2017). Article 84. https://doi.org/10.1145/3139131.3141785
12. Chandramouli, M., Zahraee, M., Winer, C.: A fun-learning approach to programming: an adaptive Virtual Reality (VR) platform to teach programming to engineering students. In: IEEE International Conference on Electro/Information Technology, pp. 581–586 (2014). https://doi.org/10.1109/EIT.2014.6871829
13. Google Play. https://play.google.com/store
14. Apple App Store. https://www.apple.com/app-store/
15. Mimo. https://play.google.com/store/apps/details?id=com.getmimo
16. Sololearn. https://play.google.com/store/apps/details?id=com.sololearn
17. Grasshopper. https://play.google.com/store/apps/details?id=com.area120.grasshopper
18. Programming Hub. https://play.google.com/store/apps/details?id=com.freeit.java
19. De Giusti, A., Frati, E., Leibovich, F., Sanchez, M., De Giusti, L.: LIDI multi robot environment: support software for concurrency learning in CS1. In: International Conference on Collaboration Technologies and Systems (CTS), Denver, USA, May 2012. ISBN: 978-1-4673-1380-3
20. De Giusti, L., et al.: Herramienta interactiva para la enseñanza temprana de Concurrencia y Paralelismo: un caso de estudio. In: XX Congreso Argentino de Ciencias de la Computación (CACIC), October 2014. ISBN: 978-987-3806-05-6
21. De Giusti, A., De Giusti, L., Leibovich, F., Sanchez, M., Rodriguez Eguren S.: Entorno interactivo multirrobot para el aprendizaje de conceptos de Concurrencia y Paralelismo. In: Congreso de Tecnología en Educación y Educación en Tecnología (TE&ET) (2014)
22. Paredes, R., Sánchez, J.A., Rojas, L., Strazzulla, D., Martínez-Teutle, R.: Interacting with 3D learning objects. In: IEEE Latin American Web Congress; Merida, Mexico, November 2009. ISBN: 978-0-7695-3856-3
23. Hesse, S., Gumhold, S.: Web based interactive 3D learning objects for learning management systems. In: International Conference on Education, Training, and Informatics (ICETI); Orlando, USA, March 2011. ISBN: 978-161-8394-87-3
24. Unity 3D Homepage. https://unity3d.com/
25. Cristina, F., Dapoto, S., Thomas, P., Pesado, P.: Performance evaluation of a 3D engine for mobile devices. In: De Giusti, A.E. (ed.) CACIC 2017. CCIS, vol. 790, pp. 155–163. Springer, Cham (2018). https://doi.org/10.1007/978-3-319-75214-3_15
26. Cristina, F., Dapoto, S., Thomas, P., Pesado, P.: Análisis de consumo de energía en aplicaciones 3D sobre dispositivos móviles. In: XXIV Congreso Argentino de Ciencias de la Computación CACIC, Universidad Nacional del Centro de la Provincia de Buenos Aires, Tandil, Argentina, pp. 622–630 (2018). ISBN: 978-950-658-472-6
27. Cristina, F., Dapoto, S., Thomas, P., Pesado, P., Altamirano, J.P., De la Canal Erbetta, M.: Aplicaciones Móviles 3D: un estudio comparativo de performance y consumo de energía. In:

XXVI Congreso Argentino de Ciencias de la Computación CACIC, Universidad Nacional de La Matanza, San Justo, Argentina, pp. 408–417 (2020). ISBN: 978-987-4417-90-9

28. Google VR SDK for Unity with Android. https://developers.google.com/vr/develop/unity/get-started-android
29. Cristina, F., Dapoto, S., Thomas, P., Pesado, P.: Prototipo móvil 3D para el aprendizaje de algoritmos básicos. In: XXI Congreso Argentino de Ciencias de la Computación CACIC 2015, Universidad Nacional del Noroeste de la Provincia de Buenos Aires (UNNOBA), Junín, Argentina (2015). 978-987-3724-37-4
30. Unity Standalone File Browser. https://github.com/gkngkc/UnityStandaloneFileBrowser

Author Index

Printed in the United States
by Baker & Taylor Publisher Services